W9-BCY-499

# Thinking Critically:
# Nuclear Proliferation

Jamuna Carroll

San Diego, CA

© 2019 ReferencePoint Press, Inc.
Printed in the United States

For more information, contact:
ReferencePoint Press, Inc.
PO Box 27779
San Diego, CA 92198
www.ReferencePointPress.com

Picture Credits:
cover: 3DSculptor/iStockphoto.com
9: Associated Press
charts and graphs by Maury Aaseng

LIBRARY OF CONGRESS CATALOGING-IN-PUBLICATION DATA

Name: Carroll, Jamuna, author.
Title: Thinking Critically: Nuclear Proliferation/by Jamuna Carroll.
Description: San Diego, CA: ReferencePoint Press, Inc., 2019. | Series: Thinking Critically series |
    Audience: Grades 9–12. | Includes bibliographical references and index.
Identifiers: LCCN 2018022049 (print) | LCCN 2018029309 (ebook) | ISBN 9781682824405 (eBook)
    | ISBN 9781682824399 (hardback)
Subjects: LCSH: Nuclear nonproliferation—Juvenile literature.
Classification: LCC JZ5675 (ebook) | LCC JZ5675 .C386 2019 (print) | DDC 327.1/747—dc23
LC record available at https://lccn.loc.gov/2018022049

# Contents

Foreword                                                                  4

Overview: Nuclear Proliferation                                           6

Chapter One: Should Nuclear Weapons Be Banned?                           12
The Debate at a Glance                                                   12
Nuclear Weapons Cannot Be Prohibited                                    13
Nuclear Weapons Must Be Prohibited                                      19

Chapter Two: Can Rogue Nations Be Deterred from
Developing Nuclear Weapons?                                              25
The Debate at a Glance                                                   25
Sanctions and Diplomacy Can Halt Rogue States' Nuclear Programs         26
Sanctions and Diplomacy Cannot Deter Rogue States' Nuclear
   Programs                                                              33

Chapter Three: Are Terrorists Likely to Access Nuclear
Weapons?                                                                 39
The Debate at a Glance                                                   39
The Threat of Nuclear Terrorism Is Real                                  40
Nuclear Terrorism Is Very Unlikely                                       46

Chapter Four: Should the US President Have Sole Nuclear
Launch Authority?                                                        52
The Debate at a Glance                                                   52
The US President Should Be the Only Person Who Can Order a
   Nuclear Strike                                                        53
The US President Should Not Be Able to Single-Handedly Order a
   Nuclear Strike                                                        59

Source Notes                                                             65
Nuclear Proliferation Facts                                              68
Related Organizations and Websites                                       71
For Further Research                                                     74
Index                                                                    76
About the Author                                                         80

# Foreword

"Literacy is the most basic currency of the knowledge economy we're living in today." Barack Obama (at the time a senator from Illinois) spoke these words during a 2005 speech before the American Library Association. One question raised by this statement is: What does it mean to be a literate person in the twenty-first century?

E.D. Hirsch Jr., author of *Cultural Literacy: What Every American Needs to Know*, answers the question this way: "To be culturally literate is to possess the basic information needed to thrive in the modern world. The breadth of the information is great, extending over the major domains of human activity from sports to science."

But literacy in the twenty-first century goes beyond the accumulation of knowledge gained through study and experience and expanded over time. Now more than ever literacy requires the ability to sift through and evaluate vast amounts of information and, as the authors of the Common Core State Standards state, to "demonstrate the cogent reasoning and use of evidence that is essential to both private deliberation and responsible citizenship in a democratic republic."

The *Thinking Critically* series challenges students to become discerning readers, to think independently, and to engage and develop their skills as critical thinkers. Through a narrative-driven, pro/con format, the series introduces students to the complex issues that dominate public discourse—topics such as gun control and violence, social networking, and medical marijuana. Each chapter revolves around a single, pointed question such as Can Stronger Gun Control Measures Prevent Mass Shootings?, or Does Social Networking Benefit Society?, or Should Medical Marijuana Be Legalized? This inquiry-based approach introduces student researchers to core issues and concerns on a given topic. Each chapter includes one part that argues the affirmative and one part that argues the negative—all written by a single author. With the single-author format the predominant arguments for and against an issue can be synthesized into clear, accessible discussions supported by details and evidence including relevant facts, direct quotes, current examples, and statistical illustrations. All volumes include focus questions to guide students as they read each pro/con discussion, a list of key facts, and an annotated list of related organizations and websites for conducting further research.

The authors of the Common Core State Standards have set out the particular qualities that a literate person in the twenty-first century must have. These include the ability to think independently, establish a base of knowledge across a wide range of subjects, engage in open-minded but discerning reading and listening, know how to use and evaluate evidence, and appreciate and understand diverse perspectives. The new *Thinking Critically* series supports these goals by providing a solid introduction to the study of pro/con issues.

# Nuclear Proliferation

In 2018 scientists made a menacing pronouncement. The Doomsday Clock, which represents the growing likelihood of an apocalypse as the time nears midnight, ticked forward to two minutes to midnight. Humanity is closer to catastrophe than it has been since 1953, experts say, because of escalating threats of nuclear war between US president Donald Trump and North Korea's leader Kim Jong Un.

To the world's dismay the North Korean regime has developed nuclear bombs, or nukes, the world's most destructive weaponry. "No nation on Earth has an interest in seeing this band of criminals arm itself with nuclear weapons," President Trump lamented in 2017. "If [the United States] is forced to defend itself or its allies, we will have no choice but to totally destroy North Korea."[1] Analysts believe Trump meant he would use nuclear bombs to decimate the country of 25.4 million people if it continues its nuclear weapons program. Soon after, the United States flew nuclear-capable bomber jets near North Korea as a warning shot. For its part, North Korea vowed to explode a nuclear warhead over the Pacific Ocean and to bomb the US territory of Guam. The world seems on the verge of nuclear war. But how did it get here?

## The Rush to Develop Nuclear Weapons

North Korea and other rogue, or unpredictable, nations have acquired nuclear bombs despite global efforts to limit proliferation. Technically, nuclear proliferation is the spread of nuclear weapons, technology, or materials to countries other than the first five that developed nuclear bombs—the United States, Russia, the United Kingdom (UK), France, and China, in that order. Alternatively, nuclear proliferation can more broadly refer to any increase in nuclear weapons or groups that own them, which is the definition used herein. How to convince rogue regimes to give up their nuclear assets is one controversy surrounding nuclear proliferation. Another major debate concerns how to lessen the risk of nuclear war in a world where proliferation is already occurring.

The first—and only—time that nuclear weapons have been used on people was during World War II. The United States dropped two cataclysmic bombs on Hiroshima and Nagasaki, Japan. Within days the war had ended, but a nuclear arms race had begun. Other nations rushed to develop nuclear weapons, and soon the Soviet Union and the United States emerged as the two nuclear superpowers. By 1986 nearly all of the world's 70,300 nuclear weapons belonged to them. They also helped their allies establish nuclear programs. But as nuclear industry increases, so too do the potential dangers of these mighty weapons being stolen, detonated accidentally, developed by renegade groups, or used to initiate war.

## The Horror of a Single Nuclear Strike

Consider the volatile situation with North Korea. Experts agree that North Korea would not attack America unprovoked, and question whether its weapons can travel far enough to reach the United States. But if their leaders' menacing rhetoric initiated nuclear war, nonproliferation expert Jeffrey Lewis predicts Kim would target New York City, where Trump Tower is located. A North Korean warhead would probably yield 30 kilotons of explosive force (each kiloton is the equivalent of 1,000 tons of TNT). That is even more powerful than the 15-kiloton bomb dropped on Hiroshima but pales in comparison to contemporary US and Russian weapons; the largest nuclear device ever detonated was a 50-megaton bomb (equal to 50 million tons of TNT) that Russia tested in 1961.

North Korea's bomb would hit before New Yorkers could be evacuated: First, people would see a blinding flash of light. A few seconds later a fireball nearly three-quarters of a mile (1.2 km) wide would vaporize everything nearby and shoot a mushroom cloud high into the sky. The fireball in Hiroshima exceeded 12,000°F (6,649°C), hotter than the sun's surface. The bomb would spark multiple fires. In Hiroshima the fires converged into what is known as a firestorm, which damaged more than 90 percent of the city's structures. The explosion's force would create a shock wave that could break glass 4 miles (6.4 km) away.

Most people within a mile (1.6 km) of the detonation would die immediately. Others would suffer third-degree burns as their skin melts away. If the warhead exploded over Times Square, science historian Alex Wellerstein estimates it would kill 700,000 people instantly and injure another 800,000. Worse, a nuclear bomb produces deadly radiation that can drift hundreds of miles, poisoning even more people.

## All Sides Agree on the Perils of Nuclear War

Perhaps the most harrowing aspect of nuclear weapons is that if one is ever detonated, the attacked country or its allies would almost certainly unleash nuclear force in return. In this case the United States would likely launch a nuclear bomb at North Korea's capital, Pyongyang. In the ensuing conflict, North Korea might attack nearby US allies—Japan and South Korea. Millions could die. As radiation spreads to nearby countries, they might strike the attacker, potentially turning a regional war into the global catastrophe that both antinuclear activists and pronuclear advocates warn about.

Notably, both sides agree that nuclear war must be avoided, and no country intends to ever use a nuclear bomb. According to the nuclear nations, their assets serve to deter attacks from each other and from enemies, all of whom fear a nuclear retaliation. Defense expert Peter Huessy explains, "Nuclear weapons were deployed and remained deployed in such a manner by the United States to make sure nuclear weapons of any kind are never used."[2] After all, countries know the US arsenal could easily obliterate them. Opponents of nuclear weapons, however, argue that these devices would not be needed for protection if all countries relinquished them.

## Nonproliferation Efforts

To limit the number of nations that wield nuclear bombs, the Treaty on the Non-Proliferation of Nuclear Weapons (NPT) was created in 1968. The 191 countries that signed it promise not to develop nuclear

weapons, and the five nations who already had them cannot provide them to nonnuclear nations. Although experts estimated in the 1960s that there would be more than forty countries with nuclear arsenals by 2000, the NPT succeeded in limiting this number to eight. That includes the five original nuclear nations plus India, Pakistan, and Israel, though Israel has not admitted that it has a nuclear arsenal. Later, North Korea became the ninth nuclear nation; it withdrew from the NPT in 2003, proving that the treaty was not a binding solution.

Since the 1990s, nuclear countries have ramped up efforts to reduce proliferation. To deter theft, nations improved security at nuclear sites that have weapons or materials to make them. The two superpowers also began dismantling bombs. Their efforts were boosted by the New Strategic Arms Reduction Treaty (New START), which Russia and the United States signed in 2011. By 2018 the two nations had decreased their combined nuclear assets by 16 percent, bringing the world total down to 14,200, according to the Federation of American Scientists (FAS).

# Nuclear Bombs Are Not Easy to Develop

Another factor that limits nuclear proliferation is the weapons' complexity. Hydrogen bombs are more advanced than the atomic bombs that were dropped on Japan. Both cause an explosion through fission: by splitting the nucleus, or core, of an atom of fissile material; that is, any material that can sustain a nuclear chain reaction. This triggers a chain reaction that causes a huge eruption. But a hydrogen bomb begins with fission and then adds fusion—its hydrogen atoms are split apart, releasing particles that then fuse together.

Because nuclear science is complicated, only countries with plentiful resources, money, and scientific expertise have developed nuclear weaponry. Each bomb requires either uranium or plutonium, both rare and unstable elements that have to be processed in complex ways. Uranium is mined and enriched in specialized centrifuges to become the highly enriched uranium (HEU) needed for weapons. Plutonium comes from reprocessing material from nuclear reactors. Because HEU degrades over time, countries must continuously make more, which impedes efforts to limit proliferation.

Other, smaller nuclear weapons have been built, though never set off. They include suitcase-sized nukes, dirty bombs, and tactical bombs that Pakistan is creating for the battlefield. Dirty bombs can be made using radioactive substances that are more available than fissile materials and may be sought by terrorists.

# Is a Ban Needed to Reduce Proliferation?

The fear that terrorists could acquire nuclear bombs—like rogue nations have—highlights another debate. Some people argue that proliferation can be limited only by outlawing all nuclear weapons. Military expert Daniel Ellsberg contends, "If proliferation in the near future is to be averted, a real commitment to total abolition of nuclear weapons—banning and eliminating their use and possession—as the truly reigning international goal is no longer to be delayed."[3] Otherwise, there is the risk of nuclear weapons being stolen or developed secretly.

Other experts think these fears are overblown. Because nuclear weaponry requires expansive resources, the libertarian Cato Institute maintains, "Nuclear proliferation is unlikely to accelerate or prove to be a major danger."[4] Meanwhile, the United States is adding at least two types of nuclear weapons to its arsenal. Trump has also advocated for nuclear armament of more countries, including South Korea, Japan, and Saudi Arabia. For America, nuclear proliferation may be the goal once again.

Knowing the immense power of nuclear weapons, no rational leader would use them—and hopefully no erratic person ever controls them. These words from US president Ronald Reagan and Soviet leader Mikhail Gorbachev in 1985 still ring true: "A nuclear war cannot be won and must never be fought."[5] Responsible leaders and global citizens alike understand that this sentiment should guide all policy regarding these devastating weapons.

# Chapter One

# Should Nuclear Weapons Be Banned?

## Nuclear Weapons Cannot Be Prohibited

- Nuclear weaponry serves as a deterrent to war and is needed for national defense.
- Nuclear war is unlikely and is not a threat to humanity.
- Nuclear weapons have legitimate uses in certain situations.
- A worldwide ban of nuclear assets is impractical.

## The Debate at a Glance

## Nuclear Weapons Must Be Prohibited

- Nuclear weapons have not deterred war, but they have increased international tension and the likelihood of nuclear war.
- The risk of nuclear weapons being employed purposely, accidentally, or in some unauthorized manner is too great.
- There is no legitimate use of nuclear force.
- Nuclear bombs are a threat to humanity and the environment.

# Nuclear Weapons Cannot Be Prohibited

"Disarmament must take into account the prevailing international security environment. We regret that the conditions for achieving disarmament are not favourable today."

—North Atlantic Treaty Organization (NATO), an alliance of twenty-nine countries

North Atlantic Treaty Organization, "North Atlantic Council Statement on the Treaty on the Prohibition of Nuclear Weapons," press release, September 20, 2017. www.nato.int.

## Consider these questions as you read:

1. How do experts explain the apparent contradiction that nuclear weapons save lives? Do you find the argument convincing? Explain your reasoning.
2. Do you agree that nuclear weapons are vital to national security? Why or why not? Cite facts from the essay or other resources in your answer.
3. Many advocates of nuclear weapons are employed by defense organizations. How do you think their background in defense might be shaping their views?

Editor's note: The discussion that follows presents common arguments made in support of this perspective, reinforced by facts, quotes, and examples taken from various sources.

When discussing how to control nuclear proliferation, some people propose to ban nuclear weapons altogether. However, this suggestion is shortsighted and dangerous. The primary purpose of nuclear weapons is to deter war, which they do extremely well. Nations avoid major conflict because they fear that nuclear force *could* be used. Yet no country aspires to use its nuclear assets. Whereas these weapons pose little threat to people, they do protect the United States and its allies from real dangers posed by hostile powers, making it impossible for the country to relinquish its weapons now.

## A Deterrent to War

Attempts to ban nuclear weapons fail to recognize that they have helped to maintain peace and save lives. Political philosopher John Gray says of nuclear weapons, "No serious military historian doubts that fear of their use has been a major factor in preventing conflict between great powers."[6] Nations are unwilling to use nuclear weapons because of what is known as the mutual deterrence theory. It states that a full-scale use of nuclear weapons between two or more armed countries would annihilate all of the countries involved by killing citizens, leveling infrastructure, and destroying the environment. Defense experts add that the atomic bombings of Japan showed how destructive such bombs are, which prevented their use—and more deaths—in future entanglements.

"No serious military historian doubts that fear of their use has been a major factor in preventing conflict between great powers."[6]

—Political philosopher John Gray

Impressively, since the advent of nuclear weaponry, the number of people killed in violent conflicts has plunged. Few nations are willing to battle with nuclear-armed nations or their allies, because nuclear bombs might be used as retribution. According to the US Department of Defense (DoD), 1.75 percent of the world's population (including civilians and military) was being killed in wars at the time the atomic bombs were used in 1945. Immediately, this number dropped to 0.4 percent, and today is less than 0.01 percent. Without nuclear weapons, the world would once again be immersed in deadly wars on a global scale.

## National Security and Defense

The nuclear nations have a right to keep nuclear weapons to protect themselves as well as discourage conflicts. Analysts Michaela Dodge and Tom Wilson from the Heritage Foundation insist, "The point of possessing nuclear weapons [is] to deter large-scale attacks against the United States, assure our allies so that they won't develop their own nuclear capabilities, and win a nuclear war should the extreme circumstance demand it." As the United States fights the War on Terror and faces potential crises with Russia and other nuclear-armed countries, it cannot denuclearize now.

Nor can other nations. Dodge and Wilson stress that the desire "to eliminate nuclear weapons from the world . . . is a completely unrealistic goal given the world as we know it."[7] In today's tense climate, countries face too many threats by land, sea, and air.

> "To eliminate nuclear weapons from the world . . . is a completely unrealistic goal given the world as we know it."[7]
>
> —Michaela Dodge and Tom Wilson of the Heritage Foundation

It follows that banning nuclear weapons would jeopardize international security. With this in mind, the nations that own nuclear weapons refused to vote on a United Nations (UN) treaty to ban them in 2017. In a joint statement, representatives from the United States, the UK, and France explain why they oppose it: "A purported ban on nuclear weapons that does not address the security concerns that continue to make nuclear deterrence necessary cannot result in the elimination of a single nuclear weapon and will not enhance any country's security."[8]

In fact, some countries may need to increase their nuclear arsenals to meet their security needs. In 2018 the DoD reported that Russia and China may be modernizing (replacing) and possibly expanding their nuclear weaponry. Defense Secretary Jim Mattis insists that the United States must respond in kind. "It is not possible to delay modernization of our nuclear forces," he maintains. "We must recognize that the current environment makes further progress toward nuclear arms reductions in the near term extremely challenging."[9] Now is the time to expand, not shrink, nuclear assets.

## Not a Threat to Humanity

Although nuclear weapons are used to deter aggressors, they do not pose a risk to people if they are never detonated. Despite doomsayers'

# Nuclear Weapons Save Lives by Deterring War

Nuclear weapons prevent deadly conflicts because countries are unwilling to wage war if there is a risk that nuclear bombs could be used. Before the nuclear age, 1.75 percent of the world's population, including civilians and members of the military, was dying in wars. When atomic bombs were used in 1945, wartime fatalities immediately decreased to 0.4 percent, and since 2000 they have held steady at less than 0.01 percent. This chart, created using statistics by the Department of Defense Historical Office, shows that the world's nuclear arsenal is necessary.

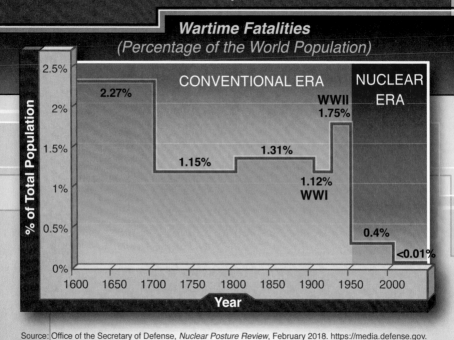

**Wartime Fatalities**
*(Percentage of the World Population)*

Source: Office of the Secretary of Defense, *Nuclear Posture Review*, February 2018. https://media.defense.gov.

predictions, no country—except the United States in World War II—has ever deployed a nuclear bomb, which makes a ban unnecessary. Furthermore, when experts caution that nuclear weapons could cause an apocalypse, they are referring to multiple bombs being lobbed back and forth between countries. That has never happened and most likely never will because nations are too wary of nuclear war. Doctoral student Mattias Eken points out that overblown fears of nuclear weapons prevent their use. He maintains, "Any posturing and exaggerating which intensifies our fear of [nuclear weapons] makes us less likely to use them."[10] But in reality, the risk of nuclear war is very low.

Similarly, people exaggerate how deadly nuclear bombs are, when in fact they do not necessarily cause more fatalities than conventional weapons do. Consider the atomic attack on Hiroshima, Japan. Tragically, about 120,000 civilians perished. However, the same number of citizens died in one day in March 1945 when US forces dropped conventional bombs on Tokyo, Japan. The conventional bombing actually destroyed the city worse than the atomic bombing of Hiroshima did, according to author Ward Wilson. All bombs can potentially kill huge numbers of people, and nuclear weapons do not threaten humanity any more than other weapons do.

On the other hand, there are ways a nuclear weapon can be used without jeopardizing lives. George Perkovich of the Carnegie Endowment for International Peace admits, "Not all uses of nuclear weapons would cause a humanitarian disaster." He continues, "A state in a conflict could for demonstration purposes detonate a nuclear weapon underground or at sea, or against a naval convoy or a desert air base far removed from civilians. It is not impossible that such use would succeed and de-escalate a conflict without a series of nuclear exchanges."[11] Not to mention that nations have exploded more than two thousand nuclear bombs in remote areas or underground to test them, with little effect on the environment.

## Legitimate Uses

While it would obviously be best if nuclear weapons are never detonated, they must remain legal for use in limited circumstances. The atomic bombs dropped on Japan are one example because they brought a swift end to the war. Otherwise, US soldiers would have had to invade Japan. In that scenario the Allies estimated that millions more of their own people would have died plus tens of millions of Japanese citizens.

More recently, a majority of Americans say they support the use of nuclear weapons in certain situations. A study in the *International Security* journal in 2017 found that 59 percent of respondents would approve of a US president's use of a nuclear bomb to kill 100,000 civilians in Iran in order to save 20,000 American soldiers' lives. The same number would still approve if the weapon killed 2 million Iranians. This indicates public support for specific uses of nuclear weapons and suggests that citizens would oppose efforts to outlaw them.

## A Global Ban Is Impractical

Finally, a worldwide nuclear weapons ban would be ineffective and unenforceable. If nuclear bombs are outlawed, materials to make them will still exist. HEU will still be required to run nuclear power plants for electricity and nuclear reactors used in scientific research. Radioactive materials are widely used, including in medical equipment that treats cancer patients. Since it is impossible to ban all nuclear materials, unauthorized groups could use them to create weapons while nations are rendered defenseless.

In addition the UN treaty neglects to address key points necessary for a ban. Safe disposal of nuclear compounds can take years, and no matter where authorities propose to store nuclear waste, nearby communities protest. It is unclear how disposal would be regulated if all nuclear weapons must be dismantled. Nor is it known how countries would be prevented from secretly producing weapons-grade (weapons-usable) materials or bombs. Because these factors have not been adequately considered, prohibition is not possible.

Atomic alarmism, the tendency to exaggerate the dangers posed by nuclear weapons, has driven the call to eliminate them. Yet peace has been achieved precisely because world powers have nuclear weaponry. Nuclear proliferation can be limited without a total ban, which would hinder America's ability to defend against hostile attacks.

# Nuclear Weapons Must Be Prohibited

"The world has banned chemical weapons, biological weapons, cluster munitions, and land mines, but not the worst weapons of mass destruction of all, nuclear weapons."

—Alan Robock, climate science professor

Alan Robock, "An Open Letter to President-Elect Trump About Nuclear Weapons and Nuclear Winter," *Bulletin of the Atomic Scientists*, November 11, 2016. https://thebulletin.org.

## Consider these questions as you read:

1. In the essay Daniel Ellsberg claims that the lack of nuclear disarmament inescapably leads to proliferation. Do you accept his conclusion? Why or why not?
2. How do nuclear weapons create conflict, according to the text? Do you agree with this argument? Explain your answer.
3. Are there any situations in which nuclear weapons have a legitimate use? Use examples from this essay and the previous essay to help explain your answer.

Editor's note: The discussion that follows presents common arguments made in support of this perspective, reinforced by facts, quotes, and examples taken from various sources.

As long as there are any nuclear weapons in the world, no one on the planet is safe. Nuclear bombs are a threat to humanity and to the environment. Their mere existence increases international tension and risk of war. For these reasons the only way to reduce the spread of nuclear weapons is to outlaw all of them. Daniel Ellsberg, a former DoD official who has become an antinuclear-weapons activist, shares this view. "Effective nonproliferation is inescapably linked to nuclear disarmament," he asserts. "Fairly soon, either all nations forgo the right to possess nuclear weapons indefinitely and to threaten others with them under any circumstances, or every nation will claim that right, and actual possession and use will be very widespread."[12]

Unfortunately, the United States and other nuclear powers refuse to consider disarmament. America boycotted discussions even as 122 nations approved a UN nuclear weapons ban in 2017. The United States has a responsibility to lead the world in disarmament just as it forged the path in developing—and becoming the only country to use—these pernicious weapons.

## Huge Arsenals Are Unnecessary

Nuclear weapons must be eliminated because there are far too many of them and they fuel conflict between countries. For decades during the Cold War, the two superpowers competed with each other to build the world's biggest nuclear arsenal. As a result the US arsenal has 6,450 nuclear weapons and Russia's has 6,600 as of 2018. College science professors Alan Robock and Owen Brian Toon explain how ludicrous these giant stockpiles are. If nuclear weapons *had* to be detonated, they ask, "How many would you have to use? The answer is, probably one. There are simply too many nuclear weapons in the world, by as much as a factor of 1,000, for anyone, anywhere, to be safe from the potential effects of even a small war."[13] These numbers must be dialed way down—to zero, eventually.

> "There are simply too many nuclear weapons in the world, by as much as a factor of 1,000, for anyone, anywhere, to be safe."[13]
>
> —Alan Robock and Owen Brian Toon, college science professors

Moreover, there will always be conflict as long as some, but not all, nations bear nuclear arms. Understandably, world leaders seek nuclear weapons to defend against other nations that wield them. Yet the nine nuclear countries, particularly the United States, force other nations to end their fledgling nuclear weapons programs. Meanwhile, they build up their own arsenals. Abolishing all nuclear weapons would help solve this disparity among nations that have nuclear weapons and those that do not.

## The Rising Risk of War

Nuclear-armed countries claim that their weapons deter war. On the contrary, history shows that weapons of mass destruction (WMDs) have not prevented aggression. Even after dropping nuclear bombs during World War II, the United States has since been attacked by terrorists who did not fear nuclear retribution. So have other nuclear states, including the United Kingdom, when Argentina invaded its Falkland Islands in 1982; not to mention that in the twenty-first century, nations face threats that cannot be fought with nuclear weapons, making them even less useful as a deterrent. For instance, countries have been attacked by cyberterrorists who launch computer attacks and elusive terrorist groups, including al Qaeda and ISIS, none of which can be retaliated against with nuclear strikes.

Not only do nuclear weapons fail to prevent war, but they also increase the probability of it. George Perkovich, who oversees a nuclear policy program, avers, "The threat to use nuclear weapons in defense raises the risks of escalation to all-out nuclear war, which would leave everyone worse off and likely cause humanitarian disaster. This is the horrible paradox of nuclear deterrence."[14] As an example, in the summer of 1998, longtime enemies Pakistan and India tested a total of eleven nuclear bombs in attempts to outdo each other. The test explosions terrified neighboring countries and drew global backlash because they demonstrated both countries' willingness to use their nuclear assets. Complicating matters, the bomb tests were accompanied by aggressive threats from both sides that increased, not decreased, the probability that they would direct nuclear bombs at each other.

## Accidental or Unauthorized Use

Equally important, a global nuclear weapons ban would also eliminate the likelihood that weapons could be detonated accidentally or illegally. A shocking report by Chatham House, an international affairs institute

# The World Has Far Too Many Nuclear Weapons

This map shows the estimated number of warheads owned by each of the nine nuclear-armed nations. Clearly, the world's nuclear arsenal is too large for anyone to be safe. There are many thousands more nuclear bombs in existence than could ever be needed or used without destroying the planet. The only way to prevent countries from competing with each other to build up huge arsenals is to ban all nuclear weapons.

## Approximate Warhead Holdings of All Nuclear-Weapon-Possessing States

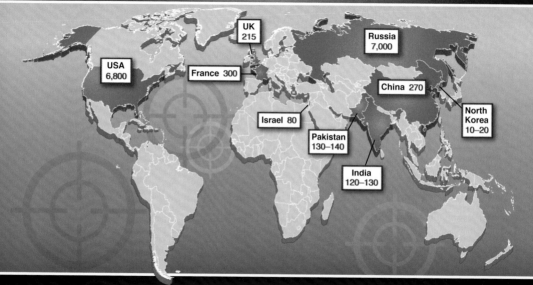

UK
215

Russia
7,000

USA
6,800

France 300

China 270

North
Korea
10–20

Israel 80

Pakistan
130–140

India
120–130

Source: Shannon N. Kile and Hans M. Kristensen, "SIPRI Fact Sheet: Trends in World Nuclear Forces, 2017," Stockholm International Peace Research Institute, July 2017. www.sipri.org.

in London, found thirteen instances since 1962 when nuclear weapons were almost fired by mistake. In several cases, malfunctions triggered false alarms. Nuclear launches were prevented only because individuals disobeyed protocol, hoping it was an error. It is also possible that a tech-savvy terrorist could hack into a system and take command of a weapon. Robock and Toon propose the solution: "The chance that nuclear weapons would be used by mistake, in a panic after an international incident, by a computer hacker or by a rogue leader of a nuclear nation can be eliminated only by the removal of the weapons themselves."[15]

## The End of Humanity

Prohibition of nuclear weapons is necessary because they have no legitimate use. Deploying these weapons would violate international humanitarian law and kill civilians indiscriminately. Each modern nuclear weapon is hundreds or thousands of times more powerful than the bombs that flattened Hiroshima and Nagasaki, Japan. Instantly, the blast could kill thousands or even tens of millions of people. Radioactive material would spew into the air, irradiating dust and dirt particles, and then air currents could spread this poisonous fallout for hundreds of miles. Radiation sickness would kill countless people and increase the risk of cancer in survivors. In this way even a single nuclear bomb can be deadly for months or years after detonation and affect nations that had nothing to do with the initial conflict.

The worst threat to humanity would be a scenario in which Russia follows through with its threats to launch a nuclear weapon at the United States or its allies. Russia vowed in 2015 to use nuclear weapons against US or NATO forces if they entered the disputed region of the Crimea, and Russia has simulated nuclear attacks on Denmark and the United States. A nuclear strike would draw the nuclear giants into a war. Combined, the two countries own 93 percent of the world's arsenal. If they unleashed all of their weapons, "They would kill billions of humans, perhaps ending complex life on earth," Ellsberg warns. "Does any nation have *a right to possess* such a capability? A right to threaten—by just simple possession of that capability—the existence of all other nations and their populations, their cities, and civilization as a whole?"[16] The answer, of course, is no.

These two nations alone could cause global environmental devastation. Setting off hundreds of nuclear bombs would so disrupt the planet's environment that it would cause an apocalyptic "nuclear winter." Robock warns, "If either the United States or Russia attacked the other with their current arsenal, it would produce so much climate change that it would kill everyone in the country that did the attacking, even if there was no retaliation."[17] The smoke and ash from fires sparked by the bombs would block sunlight for weeks. It would cause a global cooling, with freezing temperatures even in summer. Rainfall would be reduced by almost half, nearly all crops would die, and probably most humans would starve.

## Disarmament Is Required

Over the past decades, Russia and the United States have retired thousands of weapons but still retain far too many. Both countries must demonstrate their commitment to limit nuclear proliferation by leading the world toward total nuclear disarmament. Some experts predict that once countries agree to it, denuclearization would be possible within a year. Yet none of the nuclear nations has agreed to give up its arsenals.

> "Weapons that kill and continue to kill long after their use should be illegal."[18]
>
> —Ari Beser, author of *The Nuclear Family*

Meanwhile, around the world there is widespread support to abolish nuclear weapons. Two-thirds of United Nations member states voted for the ban in 2017. In short, "weapons that kill and continue to kill long after their use should be illegal,"[18] says Ari Beser, who wrote *The Nuclear Family* about the Japan bombings. Clearly, prohibition is the only truly effective way to limit nuclear proliferation and prevent senseless deaths and environmental devastation.

# Chapter Two

# Can Rogue Nations Be Deterred from Developing Nuclear Weapons?

## Sanctions and Diplomacy Can Halt Rogue States' Nuclear Programs

- Diplomatic negotiations can persuade North Korea to denuclearize.
- International agreements, such as the Iran nuclear deal of 2015, prevent nuclear proliferation.
- Economic sanctions can force rogue nations to suspend their nuclear programs.

## The Debate at a Glance

## Sanctions and Diplomacy Cannot Deter Rogue States' Nuclear Programs

- Diplomatic talks and treaties have not ended North Korea's nuclear weapons development.
- The United States abandoned the Iran nuclear deal because it does not prevent nuclear proliferation.
- Economic sanctions will not persuade rogue nations to change their nuclear policy.

# Sanctions and Diplomacy Can Halt Rogue States' Nuclear Programs

"Imagine how much safer the world would be if a [nuclear] deal had been struck with North Korea years ago, before it could threaten to incinerate part of the United States."

—The editorial board of *USA Today*

Editorial Board, "Iran Nuclear Deal Is Working," *USA Today*, July 20, 2017. www.usatoday.com.

## Consider these questions as you read:

1. Considering the ideas presented in this discussion, how persuasive is the argument that diplomatic efforts can limit nuclear proliferation? Which evidence is strongest, and why?
2. How might the US decision to withdraw from the Iran agreement increase nuclear proliferation? Support your answer with specific details.
3. Are you convinced that economic sanctions can persuade a rogue nation to give up its nuclear weapons? Why or why not? Use evidence to support your answer.

Editor's note: The discussion that follows presents common arguments made in support of this perspective, reinforced by facts, quotes, and examples taken from various sources.

Rogue states act unpredictably and lack respect for other nations. Whereas other countries have followed the letter of the 1968 Treaty on the Non-Proliferation of Nuclear Weapons (NPT), North Korea and Iran, for instance, developed nuclear weapons despite signing the international accord. Conceivably, their erratic leaders may actually use nuclear weapons on their enemies. For this reason, rogue regimes must be deterred from using nuclear weaponry—but it must be done peacefully. Only measured diplomacy and tough economic sanctions can achieve this goal.

Although some experts suggest that the United States should bomb countries that acquire nukes illicitly, that would recklessly trigger war. The majority of Americans support nonviolent strategies, with 52 percent of those polled by Quinnipiac University in 2017 saying it is more important to avoid war with North Korea than to forcibly eliminate its nuclear weapons. The United States must resume diplomatic efforts and sanctions to prevent renegade states from continuing their nuclear programs, for going to war with them is impractical and not in the world's best interests.

## Diplomacy, Not Threats

Diplomacy, which includes negotiations and treaties, becomes critical when renegade states seek nuclear weapons. With North Korea it is the only viable solution, according to the Union of Concerned Scientists. However, in 2017 the incoming President Trump embraced bullying over diplomacy and vowed to rain down "fire and fury like the world has never seen"[19] on North Korea. Many interpreted the language to mean the president would use nuclear weapons to get his way. Richard Haass of the Council on Foreign Relations predicted in late 2017 that there is a 50 percent chance of nuclear war between the two nations. Astoundingly, when then secretary of state Rex Tillerson announced that diplomatic talks with North Korea were possible, Trump dismissed it as a waste of time, fueling speculations of a coming conflict.

On the contrary, peaceful negotiations must be the goal. In a joint letter, twenty-nine experts in nuclear and foreign policy call on the US government to pursue diplomatic efforts with North Korea. They write, "The Trump administration's policy of 'maximum pressure and engagement,' presidential threats of 'fire and fury,' and demonstrations of U.S. military capabilities, have failed to . . . convince [North Korea's leaders] to trade away any aspect of their nuclear weapons program."[20] Certainly, Kim Jong Un will not relinquish weapons when he feels threatened by a nuclear giant. On June 12, 2018 Kim and Trump met in Singapore to discuss North Korean denuclearization but the brief joint statement issued after the meeting included no details and no timeline for action.

## Diplomatic Denuclearization

For diplomacy to work with North Korea, US officials must be willing to offer security, economic aid, or other concessions in exchange for nuclear disarmament. They may even have to allow the country to keep its weapons if it promises to meet certain conditions. Most importantly the United States must keep to its agreements.

For proof that diplomacy can reduce nuclear proliferation, one can look to history. Thanks to the NPT, only nine nations have nuclear weapons today. Several countries have given up their nuclear arsenal, including Libya, South Africa, Belarus, and Kazakhstan. Ukraine handed over nineteen hundred bombs in exchange for hundreds of millions of dollars and assurance that the nuclear superpowers would not attack it. Even North Korea agreed to limit its nuclear program in a 1994 agreement with the United States. That prevented the country from developing at least a hundred nuclear weapons until the deal was abandoned in 2002.

> "Missing, so far, from the U.S. strategy has been an effective and consistent strategy for diplomatic engagement with North Korea to halt and reverse its dangerous nuclear and missile pursuits."[20]
>
> —Letter signed by twenty-nine nuclear policy experts

## Iran Nuclear Deal Makes the World Safer

A particularly successful diplomatic solution is the Joint Comprehensive Plan of Action (JCPOA) created by US president Barack Obama. It was enacted in 2015 between Iran, the European Union (EU), and six other countries. Under the deal, Iran pledged to permanently refrain from "activities which could contribute to the design and development of a nuclear explosive device."[21] In return the other nations lifted oil and banking sanctions, thus allowing the rogue country to rejoin the global economy after being isolated for ten years. Preventing Iran from developing nuclear weaponry is crucial considering that it has many enemies, including Saudi Arabia, Israel, and the United States.

Impressively, Iran agreed to strict oversight mandated by the JCPOA. International regulators can visit Iran's nineteen former nuclear sites, uranium mines, and other places. As a further precaution, cameras and electronic seals at the sites show that nuclear supplies have not been accessed. If Iran protests any of these actions, the deal can be struck down and sanctions reinstated.

As of 2018 Iran was meeting its requirements under the accord, which made the world more secure. President Obama notes, "The JCPOA is in America's interest—it has significantly rolled back Iran's nuclear program. And the JCPOA is a model for what diplomacy can accomplish."[22] Previously, Iran's nuclear weapons program was so advanced that the country could have produced enough HEU for a nuclear weapon within weeks. Under the accord it would take a year. Also, Iran had nearly 20,000 centrifuges, but the deal limits them to 5,060. Overwhelmingly, experts from the EU, China, Russia, and the International Atomic Energy Agency (IAEA) that monitors nuclear sites agree that Iran was abiding by the accord. So do US intelligence agencies and government officials, including Tillerson and defense secretary Jim Mattis.

> "The JCPOA is a model for what diplomacy can accomplish."[22]
>
> —Former US president Barack Obama

## Withdrawal from the JCPOA Will Increase Proliferation

President Trump, on the other hand, claims that Iran was not in compliance and that the deal was too weak. Instead of working with allies to renegotiate the deal, he withdrew the United States from the JCPOA in May 2018 and began to reimpose sanctions on Iran. Unfortunately, this will encourage proliferation. The editorial staff of the *National Catholic Reporter* warns that "stepping away from the Iran deal won't make the world safer. It will be a more dangerous place."[23] Facing sanctions from the United States, Iran has little incentive to remain in the accord and might ignore it entirely. If Iran restarts its nuclear program, Saudi Arabia has vowed it too will acquire nuclear weapons for defense. A nuclear arms race will ensue in the Middle East, and the United States will be responsible.

# The Iran Nuclear Deal Reduces Nuclear Proliferation

Since 2015, the Iran nuclear agreement has successfully limited the country's stockpiles of nuclear materials. According to the International Atomic Energy Agency (IAEA), Iran produces no 20-percent-enriched uranium, which is one step away from becoming weapons-usable uranium, and only limited amounts of low-enriched (less than 5-percent-enriched) uranium. Therefore, Iran no longer has the ability to create nuclear bombs, proving that diplomatic treaties can succeed in denuclearizing rogue nations.

## Production and Stores of Enriched Uranium, Quarterly Data

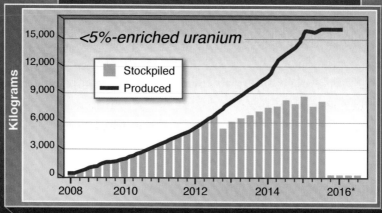

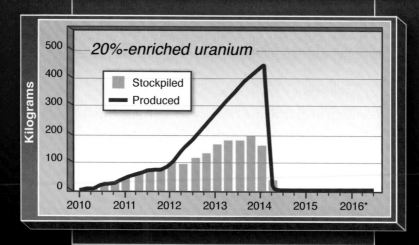

\* The IAEA has stopped updating the production figure, reporting only that any new production has not resulted in a breach of the 300-kilogram stockpile limit.

The US decision to abandon the nuclear deal may increase proliferation in a second way. The announcement angered Iran and caused consternation among EU officials and world leaders. By reneging on the deal, the United States demonstrated to its allies and enemies that it cannot be trusted in negotiations. This will hamper future nuclear agreements with rogue countries, especially North Korea. If nations give up their nuclear programs, the United States could suddenly pull an about-face and reissue penalties like it did with Iran.

## Economic Sanctions Are Effective

If diplomatic negotiations break down, countries can pressure rogue nations through sanctions—economic penalties, such as trade embargoes. Libya is a good example; it relinquished its nuclear weapons in 2003 after the United States and Great Britain implemented harsh sanctions against it. Sanctions are especially effective with rogue states that depend on the international community for survival. North Korea is an isolated country where one in three children is malnourished. In 2017 the UN enacted the most stringent sanctions yet. These ban imports and exports of certain foods, petroleum, and other products but allow humanitarian aid to North Korea.

With full support from other nations, these sanctions are strong enough to persuade North Korea to reconsider its weapons program. The fact that China is cooperating is especially important because China accounts for 90 percent of North Korea's trade, including much-needed grain and oil. In late 2017 China began restricting North Korea's fuel supply. Gas prices there shot up by 20 percent and are expected to increase, according to global news agency AFP News. China's embargo on textiles will cost the rogue nation about $742 million. Already the sanctions have shown success, as North Korea agreed to negotiate denuclearization with the United States in 2018.

## Nuclear War Is Off the Table

Only diplomacy and sanctions have been successful in denuclearizing rogue states. What does not work is needlessly provoking unstable nations. As the Cato Institute points out, "Policymakers should . . . understand that one way to reduce the likelihood that errant regimes will seek nuclear arsenals is to stop threatening them."[24] The goal should be to employ sanctions and diplomatic efforts to bring leaders to the negotiating table, not to torment them. After all, a deadly nuclear war is simply not an option.

# Sanctions and Diplomacy Cannot Deter Rogue States' Nuclear Programs

"Because the [North Korean] regime considers this arsenal to be so important for its own survival, there is no punishment the U.S. can inflict or inducement that the U.S. can offer that will make them give it up."

—Daniel Larison, senior editor of the *American Conservative*

Daniel Larison, "North Korea Won't Be Denuclearized," *American Conservative*, November 30, 2017. www.theamericanconservative.com.

## Consider these questions as you read:

1. After reading this essay and the previous one, do you think diplomacy can work to end North Korea's nuclear weapons program? Support your answer with specific details.
2. What facts presented here support the idea that the JCPOA did not adequately prevent Iran from developing nuclear weapons? Do you find them convincing? Why or why not?
3. How convincing is the argument that economic sanctions do not pressure rogue nations to denuclearize? Which evidence is strongest, and why?

Editor's note: The discussion that follows presents common arguments made in support of this perspective, reinforced by facts, quotes, and examples taken from various sources.

Although sanctions and diplomatic measures are often proposed to limit nuclear proliferation, these efforts usually do not succeed with rogue nations. Neither method prevented the nuclear armament of North

# Sanctions and Diplomacy Have Not Limited Nuclear Proliferation

North Korea is a prime example of how diplomacy and sanctions often fail to eliminate a nation's nuclear weapons program. Despite many rounds of sanctions and a diplomatic agreement with the United States in 1994, North Korea has not denuclearized. In fact, it has increased the number of tests it has conducted of missiles that could eventually carry nuclear weapons. This chart was formed using statistics through November 29, 2017, from the James Martin Center for Nonproliferation Studies and Nuclear Threat Initiative.

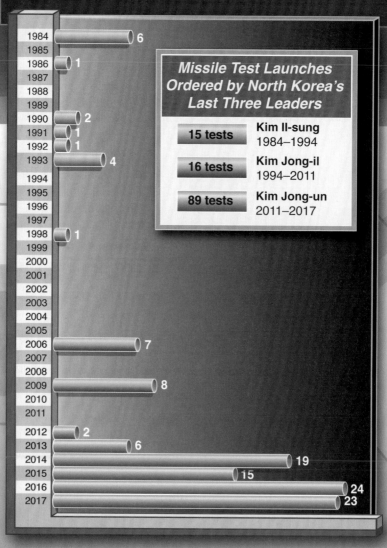

| Year | |
| --- | --- |
| 1984 | 6 |
| 1985 | |
| 1986 | 1 |
| 1987 | |
| 1988 | |
| 1989 | |
| 1990 | 2 |
| 1991 | 1 |
| 1992 | 1 |
| 1993 | 4 |
| 1994 | |
| 1995 | |
| 1996 | |
| 1997 | |
| 1998 | 1 |
| 1999 | |
| 2000 | |
| 2001 | |
| 2002 | |
| 2003 | |
| 2004 | |
| 2005 | |
| 2006 | 7 |
| 2007 | |
| 2008 | |
| 2009 | 8 |
| 2010 | |
| 2011 | |
| 2012 | 2 |
| 2013 | 6 |
| 2014 | 19 |
| 2015 | 15 |
| 2016 | 24 |
| 2017 | 23 |

**Missile Test Launches Ordered by North Korea's Last Three Leaders**

| Tests | Leader | Years |
| --- | --- | --- |
| 15 tests | Kim Il-sung | 1984–1994 |
| 16 tests | Kim Jong-il | 1994–2011 |
| 89 tests | Kim Jong-un | 2011–2017 |

Source: Eleanor Albert, "What to Know About the Sanctions on North Korea," Council on Foreign Relations, January 3, 2018. www.cfr.org.

Korea or Iran, for instance. Diplomatic deals often fail, and sanctions may actually encourage nuclear proliferation. In reality the United States must either allow these rogue countries to keep their arsenal or use military force to destroy it.

## Diplomacy Is "a Lost Cause"

Certain nations cannot be pursuaded to give up their nuclear weapons through diplomatic negotiations or treaties. North Korea, for example, feels gravely threatened by the United States, which killed 20 percent of its population during the Korean War. By developing nuclear weapons, North Korea has earned clout on the world stage and is widely feared. Former US intelligence director James Clapper says, "The notion of getting the North Koreans to denuclearize is probably a lost cause. They are not going to do that. That is their ticket to survival." He adds, "They are under siege and they are very paranoid."[25] Understandably, Kim Jong Un fears the same fate as others who gave up their nuclear weapons, including Iraqi leader Saddam Hussein and Libyan leader Muammar Gaddhafi, who were later deposed and executed.

> "The notion of getting the North Koreans to denuclearize is probably a lost cause."[25]
>
> —Former US intelligence director James Clapper

The difficulty of reaching an agreement through diplomacy is further illustrated by the absence of any specifics in a short joint statement issued by Kim Jong Un and Donald Trump after their historic face-to-face meeting in Singapore on June 12, 2018. The statement, which was supposed to be a framework for a nuclear deal, was vague; it consisted of just over four hundred words. The language was mostly taken from old agreements with North Korea. The statement said nothing about Trump's previously stated conditions: complete, verifiable, irreversible denuclearization. Nor did it mention North Korea's missiles or set dates for future meetings in which the two nations would, presumably, discuss details of a denuclearization agreement.

## Too Much Leverage

The previous scenario with the United States and North Korea highlights a drawback of diplomacy: Rogue nations may take advantage of it. Often, they neglect to make good on their pledges. In 1994 US president Bill Clinton arranged a nuclear deal with North Korea, which later reneged on its promises to abandon its nuclear program and dismantle some of its nuclear facilities. Other times, rogue states have developed a nuclear program with the intention of getting a reward for abandoning it. In truth, the United States' eagerness to find diplomatic solutions has given rogue countries such as North Korea too much leverage. "The U.S. failure to confront North Korea with anything more than diplomatic and economic sticks and carrots has emboldened the regime," says former navy captain David Allan Adams. "The North Koreans have been able to deter the United States and buy decades of time to build up their nuclear weapons."[26] Adams and other experts recommend military strikes to destroy Kim's nuclear sites.

## JCPOA Does Not Prevent Proliferation

Another diplomatic effort that fell short is the JCPOA, an accord that was supposed to halt Iran's nuclear weapons program. The international community removed sanctions against Iran and permitted it to keep its nuclear power plants. In exchange Iran allows inspectors to visit its nuclear plants and mines, but not its military bases. With these limitations, there is no guarantee that the nation is not developing weapons. Iran broke the terms by stockpiling too much heavy water used in nuclear reactors at least twice, for example, without penalty. In addition the JCPOA does not dictate how Iran can spend the billions of dollars it received when sanctions were lifted. Iran's military spending increased by 30 percent from 2015 to 2017, suggesting that sanctions relief was directed toward missiles, terrorism, and wars. House Representative Lee Zeldin from New York argues, "With too much at stake, this historically bad deal should not have been entered into in the first place and not be allowed to continue as is."[27] Accordingly, the United States abandoned the deal in 2018.

Most importantly the JCPOA did not ensure that Iran was denuclearized. According to US ambassador Nikki Haley, it is "a very flawed and very limited agreement." She emphasizes that the JCPOA was not strict enough and did not address Iran's development of nuclear-capable missiles or its support of terrorism. She contends, "We must consider not just the Iranian regime's technical violations of the JCPOA, but also its . . . long history of aggression. We must consider the regime's repeated, demonstrated hostility toward the United States. . . . At issue is our national security."[28] The agreement did not take these factors into account, and it is unlikely Iran would have agreed to more robust terms, illustrating why diplomacy does not work with rogue nations.

Even if Iran did stop nuclear weapons development under the accord, it will likely be only a temporary halt. Some provisions of the nuclear deal expire in 2025 or 2030. Former secretary Rex Tillerson calls this a "very concerning shortcoming" of the agreement. "One can almost set the countdown clock to when Iran can resume its nuclear activities," Tillerson says, "and that's something that the president simply finds unacceptable."[29] Trump wishes to negotiate a new, more restrictive deal with Iran, but it is doubtful that Iran, Russia, China, and other signatories to the JCPOA will be willing to sign one. Some experts believe war with Iran is the only way to guarantee that the nation does not develop nuclear weapons. John Bolton, a national security adviser for Trump, has advocated bombing Iran's nuclear infrastructure to achieve this goal. That could set back Iran's program by three to five years, which is more than the accord did.

> "One can almost set the countdown clock to when Iran can resume its nuclear weapons programs."[29]
>
> —Former US secretary of state Rex Tillerson

## Economic Sanctions Are Unsuccessful

Countries also use boycotts and other sanctions to pressure rogue nations to abandon their nuclear weaponry. Yet these, too, are ineffective. Years of economic penalties finally forced Iran to sign the JCPOA but did not persuade the country to stick to the terms. Similarly, multiple rounds of sanctions on North Korea did not prevent the nation from acquiring nuclear weapons. In mid-2017, the UN tried again. It barred exports of North Korea's petroleum and seafood while blacklisting North Korean workers and businesses. Although these sanctions are tough, they target only one-third of the country's economy—$1 billion of its $3 billion in trade. That is to say, they are unlikely to disable the economy. Sanctions also require the support of all other nations. Boycotts have not succeeded with North Korea because China and others fill the void.

Another failure of economic sanctions is that they have little effect on dictators or other decision makers. In North Korea, poverty and human rights abuses are rampant. Of its 25 million people, 18 million are dependent on government food rations. Limiting trade hurts these citizens but not rich government officials. Economics professor Alan Gin notes, "The government of North Korea has shown that they have little concern for the welfare of their people, allowing them to starve and live in misery while devoting huge amounts of resources to the military."[30] Consequently, he says, sanctions will not work.

Adding to these concerns, sanctions may even accelerate a rogue nation's nuclear programs. Because embargoes isolate the country, it becomes more self-sufficient and is left to develop its arsenal free from intervention. British journalist Sir Simon Jenkins contends, "Sanctions are intended to hurt an economy as a lever to induce political change. In North Korea's case they have driven an embattled regime to prove its worth by doing the opposite, militarising its society and hastening precisely the goal the policy was supposed to halt—the acquisition of high-profile weaponry."[31]

## When Diplomacy and Sanctions Fail

Sanctions and diplomatic efforts have not prevented rogue nations from developing weapons. Both antinuclear experts and pronuclear experts agree that the only other options are to allow rogue nations to retain their nuclear weapons or forcibly remove them, which may spark nuclear war. As for the first option, China and other formerly rogue nations kept their nukes—and never used them. With today's increasingly hostile environment, however, it may well be that destroying a rogue nation's nuclear arsenal is necessary and worth the risk of war.

# Chapter Three

## Are Terrorists Likely to Access Nuclear Weapons?

### The Threat of Nuclear Terrorism Is Real

- Militants could steal or buy nuclear weapons from rogue nations.
- Huge global stockpiles of fissile materials have made it relatively easy for terrorists to acquire them.
- Radicals have access to highly trained scientists to build nuclear bombs.

The Debate at a Glance

### Nuclear Terrorism Is Very Unlikely

- Rogue states would not risk selling nuclear weapons to terrorists.
- Nuclear weapons and materials are well protected.
- It is far too difficult and expensive for militants to acquire scientific knowledge and resources to develop nuclear weapons.

# The Threat of Nuclear Terrorism Is Real

"The biggest threat of all comes from the so-called radical Islamic terror groups. . . . The use of nuclear weapons, as far as they are concerned, is not off the table."

—Public policy writer Peter Roff

Peter Roff, "Rein in Rogue States," *US News & World Report*, September 8, 2017. www.usnews.com.

## Consider these questions as you read:

1. Did any facts convince you that a terrorist nuclear attack is likely? Which, and why?
2. In your view how likely is it that militants could acquire nuclear weapons or materials from rogue nations? Explain your reasoning.
3. Is the claim that terrorists have the expertise needed to craft nuclear bombs convincing? Why or why not?

Editor's note: The discussion that follows presents common arguments made in support of this perspective, reinforced by facts, quotes, and examples taken from various sources.

A grave danger of nuclear proliferation is that the more weapons and fissile materials that are transported and stored worldwide, the more opportunities for terrorists to steal them. Since at least 1977, US government studies have warned that sophisticated terrorist groups are likely to build nuclear bombs using stolen materials. Criminals may also attempt to buy weapons from nuclear-armed nations. Despite some people's attempts to downplay the risk of nuclear terrorism, it must be taken seriously.

## A Crippling Terrorist Attack Is Possible

Terrorist groups have been working to arm themselves with nuclear weapons—and have threatened to use them on the Western world. Indeed, a joint report by the US-based Nuclear Threat Initiative (NTI) and a like organization in Moscow warns of the risk of a nuclear terrorist attack. "Terrorist organizations, such as [ISIS] and al Qaeda, have openly declared their intention to acquire nuclear and radiological weapons," they assert. "Today, the danger of nuclear terrorism is real, serious, and growing."[32]

That extremists may employ nuclear weapons is a severe threat that would have disastrous results. If even a 10-kiloton bomb—smaller than Hiroshima's—was detonated in a heavily populated downtown area, it could kill half a million people instantly. In the aftermath a terror attack would trigger widespread panic and result in a flood of refugees. Worryingly, terrorists could potentially get away with the attack, knowing that authorities probably could not launch a counterattack against a roving, stateless group. Recognizing these dangers, Presidents George W. Bush and Barack Obama both called nuclear terrorism the number one threat to US national security.

> "Today, the danger of nuclear terrorism is real, serious, and growing."[32]
>
> —US and Russian nuclear nonproliferation groups

## Rogue States May Facilitate Nuclear Terrorism

One way in which terrorists could get nuclear bombs or technology is from nuclear countries. States that have signed the NPT agree to rigorously protect their nuclear assets. Rogue nations, however, offer no assurances that they will not provide warheads to radical groups. In fact, former US defense official Graham Allison contends that North Korea is much more likely to sell nuclear weapons to terrorists who despise the West than to directly use the weapons against the United States.

The idea that North Korea would arm terrorists in Syria, Iran, or elsewhere is not far-fetched, since it has already helped unauthorized groups build nuclear weapons. In 2001 North Korea sold nuclear technology to

Syria, which developed a plutonium-producing nuclear reactor (it was later destroyed). Accordingly, former secretary of defense Robert Gates claims that the North Koreans will "sell anything they have to anybody who has the cash to buy it."[33] Now that the nation is facing harsh sanctions, it is even more likely that it might seek to raise money by selling nuclear weapons on the black market.

Because rogue countries are not bound to international standards for securing nuclear weapons, it is possible that terrorists could breach nuclear sites. Of particular concern is Pakistan, which members of US Congress have called a rogue nation due to the increased activity of militants within its borders. When the Economist Intelligence Unit (EIU) of the *Economist* examined the security of twenty-five countries that possess nuclear weapons or materials in 2016, it rated Pakistan as the third-least secure nation in terms of nuclear sabotage and theft. Rahmatullah Nabil, a politician in Afghanistan, points out, "Even as Pakistani officials proclaim that their nuclear assets are secure, evidence, including internal Pakistani documents, suggests that they know better. Having served in senior roles in Afghanistan's intelligence services, I have good reason to be skeptical about Pakistan's ability to keep its nuclear weapons safe from extremists."[34] Even less secure than Pakistan are North Korea, which ranked last on EIU's list, and Iran.

## Terrorists Aim to Build Nuclear Weapons

Besides seeking ready-made weapons, terrorists are attempting to design weapons themselves. The simplest ones that they could develop are small dirty bombs, which could be made with radioactive waste from scientific research facilities or hospitals. They would not kill a lot of people; nonetheless, they would surely cause panic. Laura Holgate, former member of the National Security Council, is so certain that terrorists will attack with a dirty bomb that she says, "I'm surprised it has not happened yet."[35] In the 1990s Chechen rebels built and planted two dirty bombs meant to kill Russians, but the bombs were not detonated. A more devastating weapon is a suitcase nuke. It is unknown whether any exist, but if terrorists could create or acquire one, they could do a lot of damage. A

Terrorists could easily acquire nuclear materials with which to make bombs. The International Atomic Energy Agency monitors nations' compliance with nonproliferation and nuclear safety standards. Shockingly, it has recorded up to twenty cases a year in which criminals either possessed radioactive materials or attempted to buy or sell what was purported to be such substances. Nuclear materials stolen from unsecured sites could end up being sold to terrorists, making nuclear terrorism all too possible.

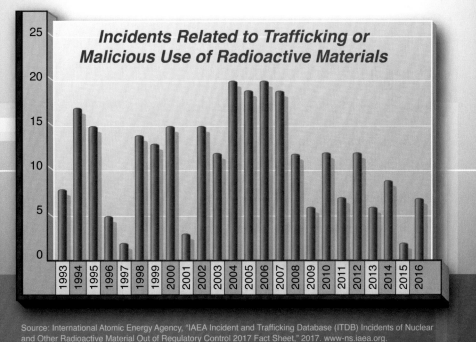

**Incidents Related to Trafficking or Malicious Use of Radioactive Materials**

Source: International Atomic Energy Agency, "IAEA Incident and Trafficking Database (ITDB) Incidents of Nuclear and Other Radioactive Material Out of Regulatory Control 2017 Fact Sheet," 2017. www-ns.iaea.org.

1-kiloton suitcase nuke could destroy everything within a half-mile (0.8 km) radius and spread deadly radiation far beyond that.

An atomic or hydrogen bomb would be more difficult for radical groups to construct and transport, but evidence shows they are pursuing it. Authorities who raided an al Qaeda building found schematic plans to build crude nuclear bombs, which are simpler than the ones that governments develop. According to Matthew Bunn and Nickolas Roth at the Belfer Center for Science and International Affairs, "It is far easier to make a crude, unsafe, unreliable nuclear explosive that might fit in the back of a truck than it is to make a safe, reliable weapon of known yield that can be delivered by missile or combat aircraft. Numerous government studies have concluded that it is plausible that a sophisticated terrorist group could make a crude bomb if they got the needed nuclear material."[36]

## Extremists Have Materials and Expertise

That terrorists could acquire weapons-grade material is very possible. According to the Union of Concerned Scientists, at least 1,700 tons (1,542 metric tons) of plutonium and HEU are stored in more than one hundred buildings across dozens of countries. Disturbingly, there have been numerous reports of security violations at nuclear sites. In 2016 alone, the IAEA tracked more than forty incidents of nuclear materials being lost or stolen and at least seven cases of criminals who possessed or attempted to buy allegedly radioactive materials. Russia is suspected of having its nuclear materials stolen over the years. In the former Soviet republic of Moldova, the FBI helped local police thwart four separate attempts made by smugglers to sell radioactive materials between 2010 and 2015. One criminal sold the element cesium, which he believed ISIS terrorists would use to make a dirty bomb. Fortuitously, the buyer was an undercover informant. Proliferation experts understandably fear that other nuclear smugglers have escaped unnoticed.

> "Even a small chance [of a terrorist nuclear attack] is enough to justify an intensive effort to reduce the risk."[37]
>
> —Matthew Bunn and Nickolas Roth of the Belfer Center for Science and International Affairs

After they get fissile materials, how would terrorists build a bomb? It would take a high level of expertise. Unfortunately, some militant groups have attracted trained engineers, scientists, and insiders with access to highly sensitive areas of nuclear plants. Probably the most disturbing case occurred in the 1990s, when a Japanese terrorist group called Aum Shinrikyo embarked on a quest to make a nuclear bomb. It managed to recruit three hundred scientists and engineers, though they were unable to create a weapon. More recently, al Qaeda leader Ayman al-Zawahiri has requested highly trained scientists to join his nuclear program.

Besides, if terrorists cannot find willing partners, they may blackmail people into cooperating. In 2015 men with ties to ISIS covertly monitored a nuclear power plant in Belgium that produces radioactive isotopes. Then they stalked a senior researcher and his family at their home. Counterterrorism experts suspect they were planning to kidnap him or a family member in order to force him to steal radioactive material. In the same way, extremists could compel specialists to help them fabricate a bomb.

## Nuclear Nightmare

In 2018 nonproliferation experts sounded alarms when the Trump administration proposed to slash $115 million from the budget of the agency that deters nuclear terrorism in America and abroad. This is a dangerous 26 percent reduction at a time when more resources, not fewer, should be directed to counterterrorism. As long as the nuclear industry exists, nuclear terrorism is possible. "Even a small chance [of a terrorist nuclear attack] is enough to justify an intensive effort to reduce the risk," say Bunn and Roth. "There is more to do to ensure this nightmare never becomes reality."[37]

# Nuclear Terrorism Is Very Unlikely

"The likelihood terrorists will be able to acquire a nuclear capacity is vanishingly low."

—Cato Institute, a libertarian think tank

Cato Institute, *Cato Handbook for Policymakers*, 8th ed., 2017, p. 721.

## Consider these questions as you read:

1. Why would rogue nations refuse to sell nuclear weapons to terrorists, according to the essay? Do you agree with this assessment? Why or why not?
2. How convincing is the argument that terrorists do not have access to nuclear sites? What piece of evidence is strongest in your opinion, and why?
3. How does the example of the terrorist group Aum Shinrikyo support the argument that terrorists are unlikely to build nuclear weapons? Did you find it convincing? Cite the text in your answer.

Editor's note: The discussion that follows presents common arguments made in support of this perspective, reinforced by facts, quotes, and examples taken from various sources.

Hyped-up reports say that terrorists are bound to launch a nuclear attack, but on the contrary, that probability is very small. For one thing all nuclear countries, including rogue nations, are too leery of extremists to provide nuclear bombs to them. Second, counterproliferation experts help keep nuclear sites secured to avert theft. Third, criminals would find it nearly impossible to gather the money, expertise, and other resources needed to create a bomb. As the Cato Institute puts it, "Terrorists are likely to continue to find that obtaining and using nuclear weapons is exceedingly difficult."[38] Consequently, a nuclear terrorist attack has never occurred nor is it likely to.

## Rogue States Do Not Support Nuclear Terrorism

No rogue nation would arm a terrorist group with nuclear weapons. Regimes have a keen interest in tightly guarding their nuclear supplies. Besides, extremist organizations such as ISIS and al Qaeda are too unpredictable to trust with nuclear weapons. They could later attack the nation, strike its allies, or transfer the weapon to someone who would.

Even if a rogue state wanted to sell a nuclear weapon to radicals, there are other barriers. Take North Korea, for example. No militant group could afford its weapons, which cost North Korea anywhere from $18 million to $53 million per warhead to make. Furthermore, counterproliferation measures would snag terrorists as they tried to transport nuclear weapons or materials. Radiation sensors at many border crossings, for instance, are designed to detect radioactive substances. Thus, foreign policy analyst Matthew Reisener asserts, "the probability of North Korea selling nuclear materials to outside actors remains extremely low."[39] Moreover if the nuclear weapon is detonated, the regime would be implicated. Through nuclear forensics, the science of tracing nuclear materials to their sources, investigators can identify the country that developed a bomb even after it has exploded. Immediately, the attacked country would retaliate against the nation that allowed the weapon to fall into terrorists' hands. In sum, even renegade states do not want ties with nuclear terrorists.

> "All nuclear nations take the security of their weapons very seriously."[40]
>
> —Stephen Younger, former nuclear laboratory director

## High-Tech Safeguards

Atomic alarmists suggest that insurgents could steal nuclear weapons. However, these efforts would be thwarted. Stephen Younger is a former director at the laboratory that developed atomic bombs during World War II. According to him, "Regardless of what is reported in the news, all nuclear nations take the security of their weapons very seriously."[40] In the United States, which owns nearly half of the world's arsenal, sites are monitored by armed guards, motion detectors, or surveillance cameras. As another safeguard, its nuclear weapons require two codes or two keys used simultaneously by two officials before they can be armed, preventing unauthorized use.

At foreign nuclear sites, security has improved greatly since the 1990s. Nuclear counterterrorism measures were further strengthened at international nuclear security summits held each year from 2010 to 2016. At least thirty-five countries vowed to follow recommendations set by the IAEA for securing nuclear facilities and transporting nuclear supplies.

## Delicate and Dangerous

Unable to buy or steal nuclear weapons, insurgents might consider building their own. For the aforementioned reasons, fissile materials are too difficult to access from nuclear sites. A bomb requires either 9 pounds (4 kg) of plutonium or 35 pounds (16 kg) of HEU, which are large amounts. Plus, fewer sites store these substances than in the past. According to the NTI, the number of countries that possess them peaked in 1992 at fifty-two and declined to twenty-four in 2015.

If terrorists did locate nuclear material, they would find it is difficult to handle. In 2014 ISIS militants managed to swipe 88 pounds (40 kg) of uranium from a university lab in Iraq. At first there was great panic that the element could be used to create weapons of mass destruction, but national security journalist Matthew Gault explains the reality: "It seemed like an army of zealots [fanatics] now could assemble its own WMDs. This was not the case. WMDs are complicated and fragile. Nuclear and chemical weapons require a degree of scientific acumen that some roving militant group such as ISIS doesn't possess."[41] As it turns out, the uranium was not weapons grade, and it was transported in improper containers, which could render it useless.

> "Nuclear and chemical weapons require a degree of scientific acumen that some roving militant group such as ISIS doesn't possess."[41]
>
> —National security journalist Matthew Gault

Another challenge that prevents terrorists from making bombs is the lethality of nuclear materials. That may explain why the insurgents did not take the deadlier radioactive substance, cobalt 60, from the college's cancer-treating radiotherapy machines. They could have made a dirty bomb, but they probably did not know how to access the cobalt without getting blasted with radiation.

## No Resources

If rebel groups manage to gather together enough nuclear material for a bomb, they would still lack the advanced knowledge and resources they need to weaponize it. Political scientist John Mueller identified twenty steps bomb makers would need to accomplish in order to fund, construct, transport, and utilize a nuclear weapon. Even if the terrorists have a fifty-fifty chance of fulfilling each task, the odds of succeeding through the final step are less than one in a million. For one thing, people train for years to become nuclear scientists—it *is* as difficult as rocket science. Extremists would not have access to engineers, nor would they have specialized tools or facilities. Plus, a bomb would weigh at least a ton and would need to be transported. Creating a nuclear weapon is such a large-scale undertaking that Mueller says only a country, not a small group, could do it.

## Too Much Effort for Too Little Reward

In the single known occurrence when terrorists acquired all of these things, they still failed to produce a nuclear weapon. The Cato Institute describes the travails of the terrorist group Aum Shinrikyo in Japan:

> Its experience can scarcely be much of an inspiration to other terrorist groups. Aum Shinrikyo was not under siege or even under close watch, and it had some 300 scientists in its employ, an estimated budget of $1 billion, and a remote and secluded haven in which to set up shop. After making dozens of mistakes in judgment, planning, and execution in a quest for nuclear weapons, it abandoned its efforts.[42]

# Billions of Dollars Are Spent to Secure Nuclear Sites from Terrorists

Efforts to ensure nuclear site security are well funded, making it unlikely that terrorists could acquire nuclear weapons or materials. The National Nuclear Security Administration (NNSA), which works to counter nuclear proliferation and terrorism, requested $1.5 billion for fiscal year 2018 alone. The chart shows how much money the NNSA plans to spend on safe nuclear waste disposal, security of radioactive materials, and international nuclear site security over the next years, including $1.1 billion to secure stores of highly enriched uranium through 2033. The more secure nuclear sites are, the less likely that terrorists can gain the means to commit a nuclear attack.

## Estimated Funding Starting from Fiscal Year 2017

| | | |
|---|---|---|
| **Nuclear Material Removal** Schedule and cost estimates | FY 2022 | $595 million |
| **Highly Enriched Uranium Reactor Conversion** Schedule and cost estimates | FY 2033 | $1.1 billion |
| **Radiological Security** Schedule and cost estimates | FY 2021 | $849 million |
| **International Nuclear Security** Schedule and cost estimates | FY 2021 | $530 million |

Cost

Source: United States Government Accountability Office, "Nuclear Nonproliferation: NNSA Needs to Improve Its Program Management Policy and Practices," Report to Congressional Committees, September 2017. www.gao.gov.

In the end, insurgents will find that it is more efficient to use a conventional bomb or chemical attacks. Aum Shinrikyo, for example, opted to use sarin gas in their tragic attack on a Tokyo subway in 1995.

Even small nuclear weapons would not be worth terrorists' effort. A suitcase nuke, for example, would require highly trained experts, constant maintenance, and a staggering financial investment. One WMD expert estimates that a suitcase bomb would need 130 pounds (59 kg) of uranium, which is too heavy to easily transport. Instead, the nuke could be made with 22 pounds (10 kg) of plutonium, but plutonium costs $5,840 a gram, according to the US Department of Energy. The material alone would cost more than $57 million. The necessary investment is too great for terrorists.

Although extremists could more easily construct smaller dirty bombs, these are not especially deadly. Circling back to the uranium stolen in Iraq, Matthew Gault alleges that if it were used to build a dirty bomb, "the effects would be nothing like the catastrophic destruction and widespread sickness that screenwriters and fear-mongers claim." It would not produce a cloud like a large bomb would, and only the few people nearest the explosion would be harmed. For groups that aim to cause widespread death, dirty bombs would not achieve this goal. In conclusion, Gault says of nuclear bombs, "The weapons are too complicated and the resources too scarce and unstable. The chances are small of a terrorist organization acquiring the materials to carry out such an attack."[43]

## Terrorists Face Many Deterrents

Besides all these barriers, fear of the consequences precludes terrorists from detonating a nuclear weapon. While they are often part of elusive groups, terrorists do have home bases in countries that might be targeted should they set off a bomb. After al Qaeda coordinated deadly attacks on the United States in 2001, its members hid in Afghanistan, prompting the United States to wage war on Afghanistan for harboring the group.

Nuclear counterterrorism measures are strong, and the United States requested $1.8 billion to continue its efforts for fiscal year 2017 alone. The fact that there has never been a terrorist nuclear attack demonstrates that the current methods of deterrence and nuclear security are working.

# Chapter Four

## Should the US President Have Sole Nuclear Launch Authority?

### The US President Should Be the Only Person Who Can Order a Nuclear Strike

- The president must respond quickly during a nuclear crisis, perhaps without consulting Congress or advisers.
- The US president's threat to launch a preemptive strike on North Korea effectively deters the rogue nation from using its nuclear weapons.
- As a safeguard, the head officer of US Strategic Command can refuse a nuclear strike order.
- Limiting the president's authority to order nuclear strikes would endanger the country and would likely increase nuclear proliferation.

The Debate at a Glance

### The US President Should Not Be Able to Single-Handedly Order a Nuclear Strike

- No one should have the sole authority to start a nuclear war.
- The US president must stop threatening a preemptive strike to end North Korea's nuclear program.
- Too many barriers would prevent the head of US Strategic Command from overriding a president's nuclear launch order.
- Congress must pass a law to prevent the US president from single-handedly ordering a nuclear strike.

# The US President Should Be the Only Person Who Can Order a Nuclear Strike

"There are good reasons for putting the nuclear authority in the hands of the commander-in-chief. In many likely nuclear launch scenarios, decisions will have to be made with extreme speed."

—David French, attorney and war veteran

David French, "We Have Enough Checks on the President's Power to Order a Nuclear Strike," *National Review*, November 16, 2017. www.nationalreview.com.

## Consider these questions as you read:

1. What are the most convincing reasons the US president needs sole launch authority, in your opinion? Support your answer with specific evidence and details.
2. Do you think that making a first nuclear strike is ever justified? Why or why not? Cite the text or other sources in your answer.
3. What evidence is there to support the claim that safeguards prevent the commander in chief from inappropriately launching a nuclear weapon? Do you find this argument convincing? Why or why not?

Editor's note: The discussion that follows presents common arguments made in support of this perspective, reinforced by facts, quotes, and examples taken from various sources.

Because nuclear weapons could annihilate the United States, the country has given its president a unique power, sometimes called sole launch authority, to protect citizens from nuclear threats. As commander in chief, the president is the only person who decides whether the country will launch a nuclear weapon. If a nuclear missile is directed at the United

States, the president may have mere minutes to respond and no time to consult with others. The US leader also retains the right to make a preemptive nuclear strike, in which a country attacks first before it can be attacked. Some critics worry that the president could use nuclear weapons illegally or unnecessarily; however, it should ease their concerns that for decades, legal safeguards have worked to prevent that.

## Quick Decisions

Sole launch authority allows the US president to respond to hazards quickly. If the United States deploys a nuclear weapon, it would be in response to some imminent threat to the country or its allies. If there is time, the president would confer with security officials, including the defense secretary and the head of US Strategic Command (STRATCOM), which counters threats to the nation. To order a nuclear launch, the president would access the nuclear football, a briefcase containing war plans and communication devices with which to authorize a strike. After providing a launch code, the US leader would send the order to military officials at the Pentagon and STRATCOM. To counter a threat in time, the president would need to do all this in less than ten minutes.

This process saves time—and lives—by bypassing input from Congress or world leaders. The president may employ weapons to persuade the opposing country to stand down, to destroy a bomb before it hits the United States, or to counterstrike the other nation before US weapons systems are taken out. David French of the National Review Institute explains that the president must retain this authority because "in such situations, decision-by-committee could lead to catastrophic delays and cost millions of lives."[44]

## First Strike Threats Are Effective

Another reason the president needs sole launch power is to disrupt other nations' nuclear weapons programs. Because Pyongyang has apparently developed nuclear-capable missiles that can reach the US territory of Guam, the Trump administration has advocated for a preemptive strike

# Most Americans Would Approve of a Nuclear First Strike

A study published in 2017 found that a majority of Americans support a first strike using nuclear weapons in certain situations. The study's authors presented a hypothetical scenario of a war with Iran that resembled the situation that the United States faced with Japan in 1945: either continue a ground war that would kill 20,000 US soldiers or make air strikes that would spare them but intentionally kill Iranian citizens. When given different options for military strikes, 59 percent of respondents would approve of a US president's preemptive use of a nuclear bomb that would kill 100,000 Iranian civilians. The same number would still approve if the weapon killed 2 million citizens. For comparison, only slightly more people would support a conventional bombing that killed 100,000 civilians, indicating that people are just as supportive of a nuclear strike as a conventional one.

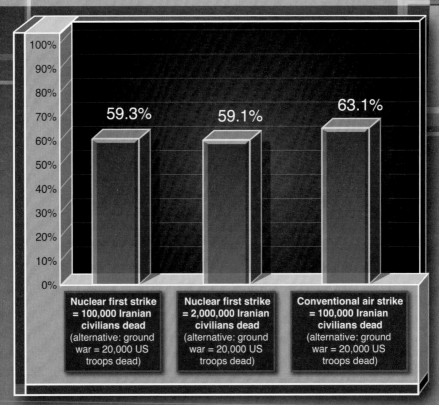

**Percent of Respondents Who Would Approve of US President's Decision to Make an Air Strike**

| Nuclear first strike = 100,000 Iranian civilians dead (alternative: ground war = 20,000 US troops dead) | Nuclear first strike = 2,000,000 Iranian civilians dead (alternative: ground war = 20,000 US troops dead) | Conventional air strike = 100,000 Iranian civilians dead (alternative: ground war = 20,000 US troops dead) |
|---|---|---|
| 59.3% | 59.1% | 63.1% |

Source: Scott D. Sagan and Benjamin A. Valentino, "Revisiting Hiroshima in Iran: What Americans Really Think About Using Nuclear Weapons and Killing Noncombatants," *International Security*, vol. 42, no. 1, Summer 2017, p. 59.

on North Korea. Most Americans support this view. According to a 2017 poll by Zogby Analytics, 52 percent of US voters say that the United States must deal with North Korea's nuclear weapons program in any way necessary, including making a first strike. America could use missiles to destroy North Korea's arsenal. Or it could threaten to use a nuclear bomb; in this case, the threat itself serves as an effective deterrent, making an actual strike probably unnecessary.

> "The moment has come to launch measured preemptive strikes to roll back at least partially North Korea's nuclear weapon and ballistic missile programs."[45]
>
> —Retired navy captain David Allan Adams

In the first option, US leaders would use conventional weapons to destroy North Korea's missile launch pads and other sites before the country can develop missiles that reach the continental United States. Retired navy captain David Allan Adams espouses this view, saying, "The moment has come to launch measured preemptive strikes to roll back at least partially North Korea's nuclear weapon and ballistic missile programs." Though he acknowledges the risk of triggering a war, he argues, "the only thing worse than a devastating war on the Korean Peninsula today is a war against an irrationally behaving, nuclear-armed North Korea capable of demolishing Honolulu, Tokyo, and Tumon [Guam] tomorrow."[45]

## The President Can Make a Preemptive Nuclear Strike

In some cases a more robust response may be needed. If a nation poses a grave threat to America, the president would be justified in using a nuclear weapon in a preemptive strike. In 2018 the Department of Defense clarified that the United States may make first strikes using nuclear weaponry. It can also use nuclear force in response to nonnuclear attacks, such as chemical, conventional, or cyberattacks. Expanding the acceptable use of US nuclear assets is necessary in this increasingly hostile world.

Taking this idea further, some experts suggest that now is the time for the US president to exercise nuclear launch authority, since North Korea is on the verge of being able to attack the United States. "How long must America wait before it acts to eliminate that threat?" asks national security adviser John Bolton. "Pre-emption opponents argue that action is not justified because Pyongyang does not constitute an 'imminent threat.' They are wrong. The threat is imminent." He concludes, "It is perfectly legitimate for the United States to respond to the current 'necessity' posed by North Korea's nuclear weapons by striking first."[46]

## Safeguards Are in Place

President Trump has made clear that his nuclear weapons' policy will be unpredictable to confound America's enemies. Although Trump's detractors worry that this means he might employ nuclear weapons unnecessarily, retired general Joseph Kellogg assures them that Trump is well prepared to solely manage the nuclear arsenal. Kellogg asserts, "I think he's got great judgment, he's got great temperament. . . . He understands the power of nuclear weapons. He understands that if you walk down that path, it's a terrible path."[47]

If a US leader did, however, make a reckless decision to use nuclear force, he or she would find that the launch authority has limits. Importantly, French notes, "it's not unchecked power. Every American president is subjected to important constitutional and military restraints."[48] For instance, US presidents cannot declare war on their own; only Congress can initiate war. Most commentators agree that a nuclear strike is an act of war. Therefore, the only time a president can legally order a nuclear strike without Congress declaring war is if there is an actual or impending attack on Americans or US allies. Moreover, it is widely assumed that if a leader called for a random, undeserved nuclear strike, the military and national security team would move more slowly and ask more questions than they would during an immediate crisis. In other words, if a president suddenly decides to lob a nuclear bomb at Canada, many more people would ask for justification first.

> "It's not unchecked power. Every American president is subjected to important constitutional and military restraints."[48]
>
> —David French, attorney and war veteran

What if a president insists on a rogue nuclear strike? The top STRAT-COM officer will refuse the order if it is illegal. Military officials are quick to point out that they will go to jail for life if they carry out an illegal strike. Not only that, but the commander would not want to be responsible for deaths caused by an errant strike. The head of Strategic Command, General John Hyten, discusses a hypothetical nuclear launch order: "If it's illegal, guess what's going to happen. I'm going to say, 'Mr President, that's illegal.' And guess what he's going to do? He's going to say, 'What would be legal?'"[49] Then, the commander and the president would brainstorm more workable options.

## Presidential Powers Should Be Reaffirmed

The president retains sole launch authority for good reason. Yet politicians have introduced bills to prevent a president from conducting a preemptive nuclear strike. Not only would that hinder efforts to defend the United States and its allies, but it would also promote nuclear proliferation. For example, the United States has promised to protect Japan and South Korea, which do not possess nuclear weapons. A law that limits the president's control of US nuclear forces could encourage these countries to seek their own nuclear weapons for defense. In fact, a bill may be needed to cement the fact that the president *does* have authority to strike preemptively without congressional approval. Senator Lindsey Graham said in December 2016 that he would sponsor a bill to this effect.

The nation's ability to fend off attacks rests solely in the hands of the elected president, as it should. Although nuclear launch authority remains an important option, it has never been used. "The fact is that no president, Republican or Democrat, has ever forsworn the first-strike capability," says former secretary of state Rex Tillerson. "That has served us for 70 years."[50] Attempts to limit the US leader's power to make nuclear strikes—including preemptive ones—are misguided and dangerous.

# The US President Should Not Be Able to Single-Handedly Order a Nuclear Strike

"No president should have that kind of power, and no president should carry that burden."

—Kit Bell, Los Angeles resident

Kit Bell, "In Defense of Trump's—or Any President's—Authority to Launch a Nuclear First Strike" (Readers React), *LA Times*, November 1, 2017. www.latimes.com.

## Consider these questions as you read:

1. What facts presented here support the idea that a president might order a nuclear strike while incapacitated or otherwise unwell? Are they convincing? Explain your reasoning.
2. How convincing is the argument that no one can override the president's nuclear launch authority? What piece of evidence is strongest, and why?
3. After reading this essay and the previous one, what role, if any, do you think Congress should play in determining whether a preemptive nuclear strike should be launched? Support your answer with facts from the text.

Editor's note: The discussion that follows presents common arguments made in support of this perspective, reinforced by facts, quotes, and examples taken from various sources.

Because a nuclear strike would have grievous consequences, it is imperative that such a decision be carefully considered by a panel of experts beforehand. However, in the United States, the power to launch nuclear weaponry rests solely with the president, which is a perilous policy. It is even more unsettling considering that President Trump, in contrast to

## Most Americans Say President Trump Should Not Make a First Strike on North Korea

According to a Quinnipiac University poll in 2017, most Americans (62 percent) oppose making a preemptive strike on North Korea before it can attack the United States with its nuclear weapons; only 26 percent would approve such an action. Moreover, 57 percent do not have confidence that President Trump can resolve the tense situation that has arisen over North Korea's nuclear weapons program. Whereas Republicans are more likely to trust Trump and support a first strike on North Korea, Democrats and Independents are less likely to.

### Would you support or oppose a preemptive strike on North Korea?

|  | Total | Republican | Democrat | Independent |
|---|---|---|---|---|
| Support | 26% | 46% | 16% | 20% |
| Oppose | 62% | 41% | 77% | 67% |
| Don't Know/ No Answer | 11% | 12% | 7% | 13% |

### Do you have confidence in President Trump to handle the situation with North Korea?

|  | Total | Republican | Democrat | Independent |
|---|---|---|---|---|
| Yes | 40% | 83% | 5% | 37% |
| No | 57% | 15% | 93% | 60% |
| Don't Know/ No Answer | 2% | 2% | 2% | 3% |

Source: Quinnipiac University poll, "U.S. Voter Support for Gun Control at All-Time High, Quinnipiac University National Poll Finds; Trump Helped Texas, Florida, Not Puerto Rico, Voters Say," October 12, 2017. https://poll.qu.edu.

previous leaders, has expressed a desire to use nuclear assets. He has flippantly asked, "What is the point of having nuclear weapons if you don't use them?"[51] and his administration supports using nuclear force against terrorists or nations that have not attacked the United States first. A law must be passed to prohibit this or any president from making any preemptive nuclear strike, or at the very least, require that other people be involved in making the decision.

## The Dangers of a Single Decision Maker

During the Cold War with the Soviet Union, the US president was given sweeping authority to order a nuclear strike in case the Soviets attacked. However, after tensions dissipated, this was not reversed. According to the Union of Concerned Scientists, "The president has unchecked authority to order the use of nuclear weapons for any reason, whether as a first strike or in a retaliatory attack, without consulting with advisers—much less following their advice. This 'sole authority' approach, a remnant of the Cold War, is both risky and unjustified."[52]

Worryingly, this puts the nuclear codes in the hands of a president who might be incapacitated, misinformed, or not mentally sound. In 1969 the world narrowly avoided nuclear war after US president Richard Nixon ordered a nuclear strike on North Korea. According to Pulitzer Prize–nominated author Anthony Summers, Nixon was in a drunken rage at the time. The national security adviser convinced the military to stand down, even though he did not have authority to override the president's order. However lucky this situation turned out, the protocol has not changed, and the military need not inform anyone of a strike beforehand.

> "The president has unchecked authority to order the use of nuclear weapons for any reason, whether as a first strike or in a retaliatory attack, without consulting with advisers."[52]
>
> —Union of Concerned Scientists

## Questioning the Competency of Unstable Leaders

Today, concerns over the US leader's sole launch power have rearisen. Many experts, politicians, and citizens question President Trump's ability to make rational decisions concerning nuclear weapons. Yale psychiatrist Bandy X. Lee has collected warnings from thousands of mental health professionals about the president. In her book about Trump, Lee warns that he has a psychological instability and violent tendencies that make it dangerous for him to control nuclear weaponry. Democratic senator Chris Murphy shares this view, saying, "We are concerned that the president of the United States is so unstable, is so volatile, has a decision-making process that is quixotic, that he might order a nuclear weapons strike that is wildly out of step with U.S. national security interests."[53] Among Trump's own party, Senator Bob Corker and other Republicans have raised alarms about Trump's threats to use nuclear weapons.

Even if everyone agrees that President Trump is a trustworthy gate-keeper of the nation's arsenal, no single person should be solely responsible for sparking a nuclear war. James Acton of the Carnegie Endowment for International Peace says of the US leader's sole launch power, "It's a genuinely important subject, and I think it's one we should be debating irrespective of who the president is."[54]

## Too Late to Stop a Launch

Some people claim that if the president authorizes an errant nuclear strike, the military will refuse to follow through. This argument does not carry weight. Although officers will not execute orders they know to be illegal, the nuclear launch process moves so quickly that they would not be able to consult with legal experts. Even if there was time, nonproliferation authority Jeffrey Lewis contends, "A lawyer may say, 'Mr. President, if you execute that option, that may be illegal, and we can have the trial in the bunker after the nuclear war.'"[55] In short, the order will be executed and the legal consequences will come later, if at all.

The only person who could supposedly stop a nuclear launch is the head of Strategic Command, but as it turns out, even that officer's order does not supersede the president's. Former STRATCOM commander Bruce Blair, who is now an antinuclear advocate, asserts, "If a president's order to fire nuclear weapons, even pre-emptively, is determined to be sound and legal, there's no one who can stop him. Not the Congress. Not his secretary of defense. And by design, not the military officers who would be duty-bound to execute the order." The commander could attempt to intervene, "but it would be too late,"[56] says Blair. The order is sent to the launch crew at the same time it is sent to STRATCOM, and it is executed in about one minute. Once fired, missiles cannot be recalled. Clearly, there are not adequate safeguards to prevent unjustified presidential strikes.

## No More First Strike Threats

At times, presidents have used their sole launch authority to antagonize other countries, which risks inciting a nuclear war. Trump told North Korea's leader via Twitter that he has a nuclear button, suggesting that he could easily unleash powerful nukes. After North Korea developed a miniature nuclear warhead in 2017, the US leader made another off-the-cuff remark. "North Korea best not make any more threats to the United States," he warned. "They will be met with fire, fury and frankly power the likes of which this world has never seen before."[57] The harsh statement stunned the world because it seemed to reflect a sudden policy change. Whereas in the past the United States promised to use nuclear force only in retaliation for an aggressive act, the American president recklessly implied he is willing to do so in response to verbal or non-imminent threats.

The US government must never preemptively use nuclear weapons, which would be an act of terrorism. Military analyst Daniel Ellsberg warns, "Just like the bombs that destroyed Hiroshima and Nagasaki, any future attack by a single tactical nuclear weapon near a densely populated area would kill tens to hundreds of thousands of noncombatants, as those did. Thus, virtually any threat of first use of a nuclear weapon is a terrorist threat."[58] To deescalate tensions, the US administration must state unequivocally that it will not consider employing a nuclear weapon in a first strike. Most people would support this decision. According to a 2016 HuffPost/YouGov survey, 67 percent of Americans say the United States should never use nuclear weapons or should use them only in response to a nuclear attack; only 18 percent say first nuclear strikes might be justified.

## Law and Order

Legislation is needed to prevent the president from single-handedly initiating a nuclear war. To this end, Congressmen Ed Markey and Ted Lieu proposed the Restricting First Use of Nuclear Weapons Act of 2017. To widen the circle of decision makers, it would require Congress to first declare war against an enemy before a president can order a preemptive nuclear strike. Importantly, this situation is not hypothetical; although the Constitution states that only Congress can initiate war, leaders have made preemptive missile strikes without repercussions. Trump authorized first strikes in Syria in 2017 and 2018 even though Congress had not declared war. Because there was no threat to America or its allies, members of Congress from both parties, including Republican Rand Paul and Democrat Tim Kaine, accused Trump of not following the law. Clear legislation is needed to prevent a nuclear strike in the future. "Nuclear war poses the gravest risk to human survival," says Senator Markey. "Neither President Trump, nor any other president, should be allowed to use nuclear weapons except in response to a nuclear attack."[59] Congress should also consider a law that requires the president to consult his or her national security team before using nuclear force.

> "Neither President Trump, nor any other president, should be allowed to use nuclear weapons except in response to a nuclear attack."[59]
>
> —Massachusetts senator Ed Markey

Many other nuclear-armed countries employ a group decision-making process before nuclear weaponry can be used. The United States must follow their lead and involve people besides the president in such a momentous decision. Citizens deserve protection from the possibility of a nuclear war initiated by one person's erratic decision.

# Source Notes

## Overview: Nuclear Proliferation

1. Donald Trump, "Remarks by President Trump to the 72nd Session of the United Nations General Assembly," September 19, 2017. www.whitehouse.gov.
2. Peter Huessy, "Why the U.S. Still Needs Its Nuclear Weapons," *Daily Caller*, August 10, 2015. http://dailycaller.com.
3. Daniel Ellsberg, *The Doomsday Machine: Confessions of a Nuclear War Planner*. New York: Bloomsbury, 2017, p. 343.
4. Cato Institute, *Cato Handbook for Policymakers*, 8th ed., 2017, p. 721.
5. Quoted in Ronald Reagan Presidential Library & Museum, "Joint Soviet–United States Statement on the Summit Meeting in Geneva," November 21, 1985. www.reaganlibrary .gov.

## Chapter One: Should Nuclear Weapons Be Banned?

6. John Gray, "John Gray: Steven Pinker Is Wrong About Violence and War," *Guardian* (Manchester, UK), November 29, 2017. www.theguardian.com.
7. Michaela Dodge and Tom Wilson, "The *New York Times* Doesn't Get Why Nuclear Weapons Are Actually Necessary," Heritage Foundation, November 9, 2017. www.heritage.org.
8. United States Mission to the United Nations, "Joint Press Statement from the Permanent Representatives to the United Nations of the United States, United Kingdom, and France Following the Adoption of a Treaty Banning Nuclear Weapons," July 7, 2017. https://usun .state.gov.
9. Office of the Secretary of Defense, *Nuclear Posture Review*, February 2018. https://media. defense.gov.
10. Mattias Eken, "The Understandable Fear of Nuclear Weapons Doesn't Match Reality," Conversation, March 14, 2017. https://theconversation.com.
11. George Perkovich, "The Nuclear Ban Treaty: What Would Follow?," Carnegie Endowment for International Peace, May 2017. www.carnegieendowment.org.
12. Ellsberg, *The Doomsday Machine*, p. 343.
13. Alan Robock and Owen Brian Toon, "Let's End the Peril of Nuclear Winter," *New York Times*, February 10, 2016, p. A31.
14. Perkovich, "The Nuclear Ban Treaty."
15. Robock and Toon, "Let's End the Peril of Nuclear Winter."
16. Ellsberg, *The Doomsday Machine*, p. 339.
17. Alan Robock, "An Open Letter to President-Elect Trump About Nuclear Weapons and Nuclear Winter," *Bulletin of the Atomic Scientists*, November 11, 2016. https://thebulletin.org.
18. Ari Beser, "122 Countries Have Moved to Ban Nuclear Weapons. What Happens Next?," *Changing Planet* (blog), *National Geographic*, July 7, 2017. https://blog.nationalgeographic .org.

# Chapter Two: Can Rogue Nations Be Deterred from Developing Nuclear Weapons?

19. Quoted in Jim Sciutto, Barbara Starr, and Zachary Cohen, "Trump Promises North Korea 'Fire and Fury' over Nuke Threat," CNN, August 9, 2017. www.cnn.com.

20. Alexandra Bell et al., "Support Effective U.S. Diplomatic Engagement with North Korea," Arms Control Association, March 5, 2018. www.armscontrol.org.

21. US Department of State, "Joint Comprehensive Plan of Action Annex I: Nuclear-Related Measures," July 14, 2015. www.state.gov.

22. Barack Obama, Facebook post, May 8, 2018, 12:37 p.m. www.facebook.com.

23. NCR Editorial Staff, "Editorial: Sticking with Iran Deal Is in Our Best Interests," *National Catholic Reporter*, October 13, 2017. www.ncronline.org.

24. Cato Institute, *Cato Handbook for Policymakers*, p. 721.

25. James Clapper, interviewed by Charlie Rose, "A Conversation with James Clapper," Council on Foreign Relations, October 25, 2016. www.cfr.org.

26. David Allan Adams, "Limited Strikes on North Korea Are Past Due," *Proceedings Magazine*, December 2017, vol. 143, no. 12, p. 1378.

27. Lee Zeldin, "Iran Deal Is Historically Bad: Rep. Lee Zeldin," *USA Today*, July 20, 2017. www.usatoday.com.

28. Nikki Haley, "Ambassador Nikki Haley's Remarks on Iran and the JCPOA," American Enterprise Institute, September 5, 2017. www.aei.org.

29. Rex Tillerson, "Remarks by Secretary of State Rex W. Tillerson at a Press Availability," UN General Assembly, September 20, 2017. https://al.usembassy.gov.

30. Quoted in Roger Showley, "Economic Sanctions Against North Korea: Will They Work?," *San Diego Union-Tribune*, August 18, 2017. www.sandiegouniontribune.com.

31. Simon Jenkins, "Sanctions Against North Korea Have Failed. End Them Now," *Guardian* (Manchester, UK), September 9, 2016. www.guardian.com.

# Chapter Three: Are Terrorists Likely to Access Nuclear Weapons?

32. Nuclear Threat Initiative and Center for Energy and Security Studies, "Pathways to Cooperation: A Menu of Potential U.S.-Russian Cooperative Projects in the Nuclear Sphere," February 2017. www.nti.org.

33. Quoted in US Department of Defense, "Remarks by Secretary Gates at the Shangri-La Dialogue, International Institute for Strategic Studies, Singapore," June 4, 2010. http://archive.defense.gov.

34. Rahmatullah Nabil, "The World Must Secure Pakistan's Nuclear Weapons," *New York Times*, April 20, 2017. www.nytimes.com.

35. Quoted in Patrick Malone and R. Jeffrey Smith, "A Terrorist Group's Plot to Create a Radioactive 'Dirty Bomb,'" Center for Public Integrity, February 29, 2016. www.publicintegrity.org.

36. Matthew Bunn and Nickolas Roth, "The Effects of a Single Terrorist Nuclear Bomb," *Bulletin of the Atomic Scientists*, September 28, 2017. https://thebulletin.org.

37. Bunn and Roth, "The Effects of a Single Terrorist Nuclear Bomb."

38. Cato Institute, *Cato Handbook for Policymakers*, p. 721.
39. Matthew Reisener, "North Korea Won't Sell Nuclear Material to Terrorists," *National Interest*, April 19, 2018. www.nationalinterest.org.
40. Quoted in John Mueller, *Atomic Obsession: Nuclear Alarmism from Hiroshima to al-Qaeda*. New York: Oxford University Press, 2012, p. 166.
41. Matthew Gault and Robert Beckhusen, "We're Scared of the Wrong Things: Americans Freak Out over Small Threats and Ignore Big Ones," *War Is Boring* (blog), *Medium*, August 7, 2014. https://medium.com.
42. Cato Institute, *Cato Handbook for Policymakers*, p. 726.
43. Gault and Beckhusen, "We're Scared of the Wrong Things."

# Chapter Four: Should the US President Have Sole Nuclear Launch Authority?

44. David French, "We Have Enough Checks on the President's Power to Order a Nuclear Strike," *National Review*, November 16, 2017. www.nationalreview.com.
45. Adams, "Limited Strikes on North Korea Are Past Due."
46. John Bolton, "The Legal Case for Striking North Korea First," *Wall Street Journal*, February 28, 2018. www.wsj.com.
47. Quoted in Jack Holmes, "A Former Lieutenant General Explains Why He Trusts Trump with the Nuclear Codes," *Esquire*, September 27, 2016. www.esquire.com.
48. French, "We Have Enough Checks on the President's Power to Order a Nuclear Strike."
49. Quoted in Kathryn Watson, "Top General Says He Would Resist 'Illegal' Nuke Order from Trump," CBS News, November 18, 2017. www.cbsnews.com.
50. Quoted in Alex Lockie, "Mattis Explains How the US Would Respond If North Korea Launched a Nuclear Missile at America," *Business Insider*, October 31, 2017. www.businessinsider.com.
51. Quoted in Andrew MacLeod, "Donald Trump Could Drop a Nuclear Bomb on Iran Within Two Years," *Independent* (London), June 13, 2017. www.independent.co.uk.
52. Union of Concerned Scientists, "Whose Finger Is on the Button? Nuclear Launch Authority in the United States and Other Nations," December 2017. www.ucsusa.org.
53. Quoted in Samantha Raphelson, "Lawmakers Fear President Trump's Authority to Launch Nuclear Weapons," *Here & Now*, NPR, November 21, 2017. www.npr.org.
54. Quoted in Robert Burns, "Trump Era Sparks New Debate About Nuclear War Authority," AP News, November 20, 2017. https://apnews.com.
55. Quoted in Terrell Jermaine Starr, "Should Congress Take Away Trump's Authority to Preemptively Launch a Nuclear Strike?," Root, November 18, 2017. www.theroot.com.
56. Quoted in Robert Burns and Richard Lardner, "Retired US General Says Nuclear Launch Order Can Be Refused," AP News, November 14, 2017. https://apnews.com.
57. Quoted in Sciutto, Starr, and Cohen, "Trump Promises North Korea 'Fire and Fury' over Nuke Threat."
58. Ellsberg, *The Doomsday Machine*, pp. 333–34.
59. Quoted in "Senator Markey and Rep. Lieu Introduce the Restricting First Use of Nuclear Weapons Act," Ed Markey, US Senator for Massachusetts, press release, January 24, 2017. www.markey.senate.gov.

# Nuclear Proliferation Facts

## Facts About Nuclear Weapons and War

- If the United States and North Korea launched a nuclear weapon at each other, a million people could die on the first day, according to Scott Sagan, an international security expert at Stanford University.

- National security reporter Jamie McIntyre told *PBS NewsHour* that ballistic submarines carry 70 percent of the US nuclear arsenal. The other 30 percent of missiles can be launched by land or bomber jet.

- According to McIntyre, a ballistic submarine is 560 feet (171 m) long and has twenty-four missiles, each with multiple warheads that can hit different targets around the globe. Each submarine costs more than $5 billion.

- Air Force colonel Carl Jones says that a nuclear warhead loaded onto a Minuteman III land missile, one of the world's most powerful missiles, would produce a blast twenty times stronger than the bomb that flattened Hiroshima.

- If one hundred small atomic bombs were set off, smoke from the fires could float 25 miles (40.2 km) into the atmosphere and affect the planet's environment for at least ten years, according to climate science professors.

- Over eighteen months of air raids, US forces dropped 157,000 tons of conventional bombs that killed more than 200,000 Japanese civilians, according to the US Strategic Bombing Survey in 1946. It says the atomic bombings killed 65,000 in Hiroshima and 40,000 in Nagasaki, though more people died later.

# Facts About Nuclear Proliferation

- According to the Federation of American Scientists, there are 55,000 fewer nuclear weapons today than there were at the peak of 70,300 in 1986.
- In 2018 the Trump administration proposed to cut the budget of the National Nuclear Security Administration (NNSA), which works to counter proliferation and secure nuclear sites around the world. Over three years, its budget would be slashed by 60 percent, from $355 million to $143 million.
- North Korea, the most recent country to acquire nuclear weapons, is the only country that has detonated a nuclear test bomb in the twenty-first century.
- Dan Zak, author of *Almighty: Courage, Resistance, and Existential Peril in the Nuclear Age*, notes that nuclear weapons have been detonated in tests more than 2,055 times since 1945, mostly by the United States and Russia.
- According to the Stockholm International Peace Research Institute, the United States expects to spend $400 billion from 2017 to 2026 to maintain and modernize its nuclear arsenal.
- Joseph Cirincione of the Ploughshares Fund, an organization focused on nuclear weapons policy and conflict resolution, suggests that the US military reduce its nuclear submarines from fourteen to four, eliminate its nuclear bomber jets, and eliminate all 450 land-based missiles. The country would have at least 320 warheads on the submarines with which to defend itself.
- Peter Huessy, president of a national defense firm, blasts Cirincione's plan. He says it reduces the nation's nuclear supply by 99 percent, from about five hundred assets to four. Plus, Huessy notes, hostiles could wipe out half the country's supply just by striking two submarines.
- A North Korean diplomat who defected told the *New York Times* in 2016, "As long as Kim Jong-un is in power, North Korea will never give up its nuclear weapons, even if it's offered $1 trillion or $10 trillion in rewards."

# Facts About Nuclear Terrorism

- According to antinuclear activist Joseph Cirincione, the United States spends roughly $35 billion on nuclear weapons each year. Yet he says the amount spent on nonproliferation and nuclear counterterrorism—in fiscal year 2017, it requested $1.8 billion—is far too little.
- In 2009 a man in Belgium passed a security background check and began working as an inspector at a nuclear reactor. Five years later, he died while fighting in Syria on behalf of ISIS, suggesting that terrorists do have access to nuclear facilities.
- In the 1990s a retired Russian general named Aleksandr Lebed admitted that Russia had recently created 132 suitcase nukes. Alarmingly, he said that dozens of them had gone missing and perhaps were in the hands of terrorists. Russia denied the claims.

# Public Opinions About Nuclear Weapons

- According to Stanford scholar Scott Sagan, a 1945 poll found that 85 percent of Americans said they approved of the United States' use of atomic bombs on Japan. By 2015 only 46 percent of survey respondents supported the decision.
- A HuffPost/YouGov survey in 2016 found that 45 percent of Americans support reducing the country's nuclear arsenal, compared to 40 percent who do not.
- According to a 2017 poll by Quinnipiac University, launching a preemptive strike against North Korea in order to end its nuclear program is supported by 46 percent of Republicans. Only 41 percent of the GOP opposes. Among Democrats, 16 percent support and 77 percent oppose.
- A *60 Minutes/Vanity Fair* survey in November 2014 revealed that nuclear war was the number one threat that people most fear will end humanity. It was named by 35 percent of respondents.

# Related Organizations and Websites

**American Nuclear Society (ANS)**
555 N. Kensington Ave.
La Grange Park, IL 60526
website: www.ans.org

ANS is an international scientific organization that promotes nuclear science and technology on behalf of its engineers, scientists, educators, and other members. Its Center for Nuclear Science and Technology Information for K–12 students provides a wealth of information on nuclear technology, nuclear science, power plant cybersecurity, and careers.

**Arms Control Association (ACA)**
1200 Eighteenth St. NW, Suite 1175
Washington, DC 20036
website: www.armscontrol.org

Since 1971, the nonpartisan ACA has provided commentary and analysis in support of effective arms control policies and agreements. It offers fact sheets, white papers, and issue briefs, such as "Nuclear Restraint Agreements Under Serious Threat." Its magazine, *Arms Control Today*, has numerous articles on nuclear weapons and proliferation.

**Beyond Nuclear**
6930 Carroll Ave., Suite 400
Takoma Park, MD 20912
website: www.beyondnuclear.org

Beyond Nuclear campaigns for the elimination of all nuclear weapons and power plants by providing information to the public, government officials, and the media about their dangers. The Nuclear Weapons section of its website covers nuclear proliferation and the risk of nuclear winter through news articles and blog posts, including "Who's Minding the Nukes?" The group also posts fact sheets, pamphlets, reports, and videos.

## International Atomic Energy Agency (IAEA)

1 United Nations Plaza, Room DC-1-1155
New York, NY 10017
website: www.iaea.org

As part of the United Nations, the IAEA helps member states and partners pursue safe nuclear technology and maintain compliance with the NPT. It publishes books, bulletins, and informational circulars on topics such as nuclear security forensics and countering nuclear smuggling. Its website also has speech transcripts, including its director's remarks on developing safe nuclear technology and facilities.

## Project Ploughshares

140 Westmount Rd. N.
Waterloo, ON N2l 3G6 Canada
website: www.ploughshares.ca

Project Ploughshares advocates for disarmament and peaceful resolution of conflicts with the goal of eliminating the dangers posed by nuclear weaponry. Newsletters, fact sheets, annual reports, and more are available on the organization's website.

## Union of Concerned Scientists (UCS)

2 Brattle Sq.
Cambridge, MA 02238
website: www.ucsusa.org

The UCS is a nonprofit alliance of scientists that examines the impact of nuclear technology on society and monitors the security and safety risks of nuclear power plants. The UCS publishes reports on nonproliferation, the *Nucleus* newsletter, and *Catalyst* magazine.

**US Department of Defense (DoD)**

1400 Defense Pentagon
Washington, DC 20301
website: www.defense.gov

As America's oldest and largest government agency, the DoD is charged with providing military forces to areas where they are needed to preserve national security. Its STRATCOM division deters attacks on the nation and coordinates missile and nuclear strikes. The DoD website provides copies of its *Nuclear Posture Review* reports, fact sheets on modernization of the nuclear arsenal, and a video from STRATCOM about strategic deterrence before and after the advent of nuclear weapons.

**US Nuclear Regulatory Commission (NRC)**

Washington, DC 20555
website: www.nrc.gov

Created in 1974, the NRC regulates and inspects nuclear power plants to ensure that radioactive materials are being used, stored, and disposed of safely. It publishes fact sheets on dirty bombs, nuclear security, and other related topics.

# For Further Research

## Books

Ari Beser, *The Nuclear Family*. USA: CreateSpace, 2015.

Daniel Ellsberg, *The Doomsday Machine: Confessions of a Nuclear War Planner*. New York: Bloomsbury, 2017.

Jeffrey A. Larsen and Kerry M. Kartchner, eds., *On Limited Nuclear War in the 21st Century*. Stanford, CA: Stanford University Press, 2014.

Noel Merino, ed., *Current Controversies: Nuclear Proliferation*. Farmington Hills, MI: Greenhaven, 2016.

Ozzie Paez, *Decision Making in a Nuclear Middle East: Lessons from the Cold War*. Fort Collins, CO: Decisions to Lead, 2016.

Brad Roberts, *The Case for U.S. Nuclear Weapons in the 21st Century*. Stanford, CA: Stanford University Press, 2015.

Todd S. Sechser and Matthew Fuhrmann, *Nuclear Weapons and Coercive Diplomacy*. Cambridge, UK: Cambridge University Press, 2017.

Dan Zak, *Almighty: Courage, Resistance, and Existential Peril in the Nuclear Age*. New York: Blue Rider, 2016.

## Internet Sources

Matthew Bunn et al., *Preventing Nuclear Terrorism: Continuous Improvement or Dangerous Decline?* Cambridge, MA: Project on Managing the Atom, Belfer Center for Science and International Affairs at Harvard, March 2016. www.belfercenter.org/sites/default/files/legacy/files/Preven tingNuclearTerrorism-Web%202.pdf.

Michaela Dodge, "The Trump Administration's Nuclear Weapons Policy: First Steps," Heritage Foundation, November 30, 2016. www.heritage.org/defense/report/the-trump-administrations-nuclear-weapons-policy-first-steps.

Greg Myre, "Giving Up Nuclear Weapons: It's Rare, but It's Happened," *All Things Considered*, NPR, May 8, 2017. www.npr.org/sections/parallels/2017/05/08/526078459/giving-up-nuclear-weapons-its-rare-but-its-happened.

Office of the Secretary of Defense, *Nuclear Posture Review*, February 2018. https://media.defense.gov/2018/Feb/02/2001872886/-1/-1/1/2018-Nuclear-Posture-Review-Final-Report.pdf.

George Perkovich, "The Nuclear Ban Treaty: What Would Follow?," Carnegie Endowment for International Peace, May 2017. https://carnegieendowment.org/2017/05/31/nuclear-ban-treaty-what-would-follow-pub-70136.

Scott D. Sagan, "The Korean Missile Crisis: Why Deterrence Is Still the Best Option," *Foreign Affairs*, November/December 2017. www.foreignaffairs.com/articles/north-korea/2017-09-10/korean-missile-crisis.

Roger Showley, "Economic Sanctions Against North Korea: Will They Work?," *San Diego Union-Tribune*, August 18, 2017. www.sandiegouniontribune.com/business/economy/sd-fi-econometer20aug17-htmlstory.html.

Terrell Jermaine Starr, "Should Congress Take Away Trump's Authority to Pre-emptively Launch a Nuclear Strike?," Root, November 18, 2017. www.theroot.com/should-congress-take-away-trump-s-authority-to-pre-empt-1820546098.

# Index

*Note: Boldface page numbers indicate illustrations.*

Acton, James, 62
Adams, David Allan, 36, 56
AFP News, 31
Allison, Graham, 41
al Qaeda, 21, 45
American Nuclear Society (ANS), 71
Arms Control Association (ACA), 71
Aum Shinrikyo, 44–45, 49, 50

Bell, Kit, 59
Beser, Ari, 24
Beyond Nuclear, 71–72
Blair, Bruce, 62
Bolton, John, 37, 57
Bunn, Matthew, 43–44, 45
Bush, George W., 41

casualties
  estimated potential, from nuclear attack
    on New York City, 8
  from attack on Hiroshima, 17
  potential, from nuclear war between
    North Korea/US, 68
  from wars, before/after development of
    atom bomb, 14, **16**
Cato Institute, 11, 32, 46, 49
Chatham House, 21–22
Cirincione, Joseph, 69, 70
Clapper, James, 35
Clinton, Bill, 36
Corker, Bob, 62

denuclearization
  debate over, 12
  diplomatic, 28
  is impractical, 18

is needed to avert nuclear proliferation,
  10, 24
United States refuses to consider, 20
would jeopardize international security,
  14–15
Department of Defense, US (DOD), 14,
  15, 56, 73
Department of Energy, US, 51
diplomacy
  can deter rogue nations from
    developing nuclear weapons, 27, 28
  with North Korea, has not deterred
    nuclear weapons program, **34,** 35, 36
dirty bombs, 10
  attempts by Chechen rebels to use, 42
Dodge, Michaela, 14–15
Doomsday Clock, 6

economic sanctions
  have been effective, 31
  on Iran, 28–29
  on North Korea, have not deterred
    nuclear weapons program, **34,** 37–38
*Economist* (magazine), 42
Economist Intelligence Unit (EIU), 42
Eken, Mattias, 16–17
Ellsberg, Daniel, 10, 19–20, 23, 63
environmental effects, of multiple
  nuclear strikes, 23–24, 68

Falkland Islands war (1982), 21
Federation of American Scientists (FAS),
  9, 69
French, David, 53, 54, 57

Gaddhafi, Muammar, 35
Gates, Robert, 42
Gault, Matthew, 48, 51 [ED: in italics?]
Gin, Alan, 38

Gorbachev, Mikhail, 11
Graham, Lindsey, 58
Gray, John, 14

Haass, Richard, 27
Haley, Nikki, 36–37
highly enriched uranium (HEU), 10, 18
  amount needed for bomb, 48
  amount stored worldwide, 44
Hiroshima, 7
  causalities from attack on, 17
  deaths from atomic bombing of, 68
Holgate, Laura, 42
Huessy, Peter, 8, 69
Hussein, Saddam, 35
hydrogen bombs, 10
Hyten, John, 58

India, nuclear testing by, 21
International Atomic Energy Agency
  (IAEA), 29, 30, 44, 48, 72
*International Security* (journal), 17–18
Iran
  nuclear deal with, has made world safer,
    28–29
  public support for nuclear strike on,
    17–18, **55**
ISIS, 44, 45, 48

Jenkins, Simon, 38
Joint Comprehensive Plan of Action
  (JCPOA), 28
  does not prevent proliferation, 36–37
  reduces nuclear proliferation, **30**
  withdrawal from, will increase
    proliferation, 29, 31
Jones, Carl, 68

Kaine, Tim, 64
Kellogg, Joseph, 57
Kim Jong Un, 6, 27, 34, 35, 69

Larison, Daniel, 33
Lebed, Aleksandr, 70
Lee, Bandy X., 61–62
Lewis, Jeffrey, 7, 62

Libya, 31
Lieu, Ted, 63–64

Markey, Ed, 63–64
Mattis, Jim, 15
McIntyre, Jamie, 68
Mueller, John, 49
Murphy, Chris, 62

Nagasaki, 7
  deaths from atomic bombing of, 68
*National Catholic Reporter* (newspaper),
  29
National Nuclear Security
  Administration (NNSA), 50
  proposed cut in funding by Trump
    administration, 45, 69
New Strategic Arms Reduction Treaty
  (New START), 9
New York City, potential impact of
  nuclear attack on, 7–8
Nixon, Richard, 61
North Atlantic Treaty Organization
  (NATO), 13
  threat by Russia to use nuclear weapons
    against, 23
North Korea
  economic sanctions on, are effective, 31
  impact of nuclear war between US and,
    7–8
  is not likely to support nuclear
    terrorism, 47
  launch of intercontinental ballistic
    missile by, **9**
  missile test launches by, **34**
  public confidence in President Trump
    to deal with, **60**
  public support for nuclear strike on, 56
*Nuclear Family, The* (Beser), 24
nuclear proliferation, 6–7
  abolition of nuclear weapons needed to
    avert, 10, 24
  US policy and, 11
  withdrawal from Iran nuclear
    agreement will increase, 29, 31
Nuclear Regulatory Commission, US

(NRC), 73
nuclear terrorism
  debate over likelihood of, 39
  deterrence efforts
    proposed cut by Trump
      administration, 45
    US spending on, 51
  rogue nations do not support, 47
  rogue nations may facilitate, 41–42
nuclear tests, 17
  by India/Pakistan, 21
  by North Korea, **34**
  total number of, 69
Nuclear Threat Initiative (NTI), 41, 48
nuclear weapon(s)
  complexity of, 10
  debate over terrorists' access to, 39
  as deterrent to war, 14
  first attack using, 7
  have not prevented wars, 21
  pose threat to humanity, 23–24
  risk of accidental use of, 21–23
  save lives by deterring war, **16**
  *See also* denuclearization; preemptive
    strike
nuclear winter, 23–24

Obama, Barack, 28, 29, 41
opinion polls. *See* surveys

Pakistan
  nuclear testing by, 21
  security of nuclear stockpile of, 42
Paul, Rand, 64
Perkovich, George, 17, 21
plutonium
  amount needed for bomb, 48
  amount stored worldwide, 44
  cost of, 51
polls. *See* surveys
preemptive strike
  authority of president to launch, 54,
    56–57
    proposed legislation to restrict, 63–64
  public support of, 63
    on Iran, **55**

on North Korea, 56, **60,** 70
Project Ploughshares, 72

radioactive materials
  amount spent to secure, **50**
  incidents related to trafficking/
    malicious use of, **43**
  *See also* highly enriched uranium;
    plutonium
Reagan, Ronald, 11
Reisener, Matthew, 47
Restricting First Use of Nuclear Weapons
  Act (proposed, 2017), 63–64
Robock, Alan, 19, 20, 22–23, 24
Roff, Peter, 40
rogue nations
  debate over deterring nuclear weapons
    development by, 25
  economic sanctions on
    are effective, 31
    are not effective, 37–38
  may facilitate nuclear terrorism, 41–42
Roth, Nickolas, 43–44, 45
Russia
  suitcase bombs created by, 70
  threat to use nuclear weapon against
    US/NATO, 23

Sagan, Scott, 68, 70
sole launch authority, of president
  dangers of, 61
  debate over, 52
  is needed to protect US, 53–54
  to launch preemptive strike, 54, 56–57
    proposed legislation to restrict, 63–64
  safeguards against illegal strike and,
    57–58
Soviet Union, nuclear arms race and, 7
Stockholm International Peace Research
  Institute, 69
suitcase bombs, 10, 42–43
  amount of nuclear material needed for,
    50–51
  number created by Russia, 70
Summers, Anthony, 61
surveys, 70

on avoiding war *vs.* eliminating North
    Korean weapons, 27
on confidence in President Trump to
    handle situation with North Korea, **60**
on support for nuclear strike/
    preemptive strike, 63
    on Iran, 17–18, **55**
    on North Korea, 56, **60,** 70

tactical bombs, 10
terrorist groups, are not deterred by
    nuclear weapons, 21
Tillerson, Rex, 27, 37, 58
Toon, Owen Brian, 20, 22–23
Treaty on the Non-Proliferation of
    Nuclear Weapons (NPT, 1968), 8–9,
    26
Trump, Donald/Trump administration,
    6, 11, 27, 63
    concerns of mental health professionals
        about, 61–62
    nuclear weapons policy of, 57
    poll on confidence in, to handle
        situation with North Korea, **60**
    preemptive strike, position on, 54, 56,
        64
    proposed cut in nuclear terrorism
        deterrence by, 45, 69
    on use of nuclear weapons, 59–60
    withdrawal from Iran nuclear accord by,
        29, 31

Union of Concerned Scientists (UCS),
    27, 61, 72

on amount of plutonium/HEU stored
    worldwide, 44
United States
    impact of nuclear war between North
        Korea and, 7–8
    nuclear arms race and, 7
    refuses to consider disarmament, 20
    spending by
        to modernize nuclear arsenal, 69
        on nuclear counterterrorism measures,
            51, 70
    threat by Russia to use nuclear weapons
        against, 23
    withdrawal from Iran nuclear
        agreement by, 29, 31
uranium, 10
*USA Today* (newspaper), 26

warheads
    holdings of, by nuclear-weapon
        possessing states, **22**
    North Korean
        cost to produce, 47
        probable yield of, 7
    on US submarines, 69
Wellerstein, Alex, 8
Wilson, Tom, 14–15
Wilson, Ward, 17

Younger, Stephen, 47

Zak, Dan, 68
al-Zawahiri, Ayman, 45

# About the Author

Jamuna Carroll has a bachelor's degree in writing and mass communication. Her writing appears in more than forty books on science, math, civil liberties, and history, as well as humor books. Her editions for ReferencePoint Press include *Thinking Critically: Social Networking* and *Thinking Critically: Cybercrime*. Carroll performs at storytelling events and comedy shows in Southern California, where she shares a vintage house with her partner, daughter, and two cats.